J. R. Howlett
15 August 1977
$7.97 Hugg

CP
B 564

Kent State University
Institute for Bibliography & Editing

Feb, 1946
F. R. Cooper.

BOOKS AND BOOK-COLLECTORS

By the same author

TASTE AND TECHNIQUE IN BOOK-COLLECTING
The Sandars Lectures, 1947

BINDING VARIANTS IN ENGLISH PUBLISHING

MORE BINDING VARIANTS

PUBLISHER'S CLOTH
An Outline History

ABC FOR BOOK-COLLECTORS

With Graham Pollard

AN ENQUIRY INTO CERTAIN NINETEENTH-
CENTURY PAMPHLETS

THE FIRM OF CHARLES OTTLEY, LANDON & CO
Footnote to An Enquiry

With John Sparrow

A. E. HOUSMAN
An Annotated Hand-List

BOOKS AND
BOOK-COLLECTORS

BY

JOHN CARTER

RUPERT HART-DAVIS
SOHO SQUARE LONDON
1956

First published 1956
Second impression 1956

Printed in Great Britain by Butler & Tanner Ltd., Frome and London

To my godsons
John Murray VII
of Albemarle Street
and
Giles Munby
of Cambridge

CONTENTS

CONTENTS

5. *One Bibliographical Sermon*

6. *Two Frivolities*

PREFACE

ABSENCE is said to make the heart grow fonder. After nearly three years' absence from the rare book business, and just before my return to it, I looked through the mass (as it seemed to me) of articles, essays, reviews and other similar by-products of my professional career during the previous quarter of a century. I was impressed by the number of words, but saddened by the essentially ephemeral quality of most of them; and with the best will in the world (for which of us is not pleased by his publisher's professed enthusiasm?) I could not find much that seemed to me worth reprinting.

The present selection includes one or two pieces for which I must, indeed, confess to a certain fondness. *Collecting Detective Fiction*, for instance, is terribly out of date in the light of modern concentration on the subject; yet as an exercise in machete-work through what was in 1934 practically virgin jungle, a pioneer need not perhaps be ashamed of it. Then, the ambiguous review of my own book, *ABC for Book-Collectors*, which that puckish character Edmond Segrave commissioned from me for the *Bookseller*, will always have a wry charm for at least one reader (myself) from the fact that a surprising number of innocent persons failed to see that it was meant to be a joke and telephoned to the book's publisher, Mr. Hart-Davis, commiserating with him on the terrible slating which that mischievous fellow Carter had given a book by one of his authors. I was tempted to include a tremendously pontifical *TLS* article of 1948 entitled *The Heritage of Culture*, which (I was later told, quite unofficially) became paper number one in the Treasury file whence emerged the Waverley Committee and its now famous Report on the Export of Works of Art: but why recall beach-heads after the armistice has been signed?

In the main, however, this is a conventional choice, comprising that five or ten per cent of my contributions to periodicals or collections which have dealt, however imperfectly, either with themes of some continuing interest or with persons to whom I should wish to do honour in more permanent form. I share my publisher's indebtedness, for permission to reprint, to the Times Publishing Company; to the editors of the *Colophon* and the *New Colophon* (New York), of the *Atlantic Monthly* (Boston), of the *Spectator*, of the *Connoisseur* and of the *Bookseller*; to Messrs Constable, Messrs Cassell and the University of Illinois Press; and to the British Broadcasting Corporation. The second of the two articles on the Wise forgeries was a joint product of the original collaboration; and the reader will surely share my own appreciation of Mr. Graham Pollard's amiable readiness to allow it to reappear in a book of mine.

I have silently corrected a few errors of fact, such as wrong dates. I have made a few verbal adjustments and excisions, mostly where some phrase or reference adverted, now meaninglessly, to the original circumstances of publication, and I have added to such footnotes as it seemed useful to retain. All the articles reprinted from *The Times Literary Supplement* (save only No. II of Part Four) were originally unsigned; but one or two of the adjustments above mentioned violate that traditional anonymity.

INTRODUCTION [1]

BOOK-COLLECTING is at once the most various, the most sophisticated, and the least income-taxing of the major forms of connoisseurship.

It is true that a Gutenberg Bible or a First Quarto of *The Duchess of Malfi* or a large-paper copy of the first edition of *Gulliver's Travels* costs much more than most of us can afford. But compare, for instance, the *editio princeps* of Homer, a first edition of *Lycidas* or *Le Rouge et le Noir* with Poussin or Lamerie or Riesener (to look no higher), and it becomes immediately apparent that book-collecting, even on a fairly lordly scale, is a positively economical indulgence by comparison with most of its competitors for the connoisseur's attention. It is therefore useful for those, not already addicted, who judge it by the occasional newspaper reports of the sale of a First Folio or a set of Audubon's *Birds of America*, to be reminded that an enjoyable and rewarding and significant library can be formed for the price of either of these books by a man of taste and intelligence.

The variety of book-collecting, indeed, is almost infinite: for there are books about every subject under the sun, books of every physical kind, shape and size, books in a profusion which has steadily increased from the 38,000 or so editions recorded before 1500—that is, the output of the first forty-five years of printing—to the 18,066 new books and new editions published in Great Britain alone during the single year 1951. Far too many laymen equate bibliophily with the accumulation of first editions, and first editions of pure literature at that. One of the most instructive collections within my own acquaintance was of second

[1] Originally contributed to *The Concise Encyclopaedia of Antiques* (London and New York, The Connoisseur, 1954).

editions, which (its owner reasonably considered) told us more about their author's effect on the public than the firsts, besides being in many cases much harder to find—an attraction rather than a deterrent to the true believer. It is perhaps twenty years too late to expect to assemble *for a song* a collection of original editions illustrating the development of the romance of chivalry, of electricity, of the Victorian novel, of African exploration, of Italian opera, or of the detective story. But the history of mountaineering, of art criticism, of nuclear fission; English hymnwriters, the minor Romantic poets, the Edwardian novelists; Renaissance latinity, the Oxford Movement, Mr. Wise's forgeries; baroque book-design, the illustrators between Bewick and the sixties, distinguished printing between Kelmscott and Nonesuch; chancery-style italic, eighteenth-century Irish bindings, non-fiction issued in serial parts—it would be easy to fill a couple of pages with inviting and only partially explored fields. The complaint is often heard that the supply of desirable books is drying up, that everything has gone to America, that all the fine things gravitate to public or academic libraries, whence they can never emerge. It is true that even a millionaire would be ill advised today to start collecting Elizabethan drama or the *editiones principes* of the Greek and Latin classics with any serious expectation of achieving completeness. Yet history has shown (so far) that for every section of obvious foreground that becomes hopelessly overrun, at least two enticing vistas open up in the middle distance.

This limitless potentiality for the expansion of interest —for the relating of unconsidered books to some instructive or attractive pattern of collecting—is based upon the threefold nature of bibliophily's appeal. For a book may appeal to the eye, by its beauty or singularity of printing, illustration or binding; it may appeal to the intellect, by the power, influence, or significance of its content; or it may appeal to the imagination, to that sense of the past which is active in some of us, latent in all of us—the emotion evoked as sharply by the dim, scrubby print of Pascal's *Les Provinciales* or *The Pilgrim's Progress* or *The Communist Manifesto* in their original form as by the elegance of Gray's *Elegy* or *Adonais* in theirs—the feeling that, whether we care about first editions or not, Pope should be read in folio, Gibbon in quarto and Jane Austen in small octavo. And to whichever aspect of this fundamental variety may attract the collector is added the third quality claimed in the opening sentence of this note: a range of technical connoisseurship as sophisticated, as esoteric and as minute as could be demanded by the most exacting devotee of prints or silver, china or furniture. If books are not always as prolific of "states" as some prints; if hallmarks can be trickier than colophons; if an imitative porcelain factory can cause as much initial confusion as a piratical publisher; if chairs are more often "restored" than *incunabula* are "made-up"; nevertheless, books can hold their own with any competitors for an all-round standard of delicate nicety in the sphere of collecting technique.

PART ONE

Seven Book-Collectors

THOMAS J. WISE [1]

By the death of Thomas J. Wise the world of books (which is a different place from the literary world) loses one of its best known and at the same time most enigmatic figures. Wise had been President of the Bibliographical Society, and was on its Council for many years: he was a member of the Roxburghe Club, the most aristocratic and exclusive of all book-collecting fraternities: he was an honorary Master of Arts of Oxford University and a Fellow of Worcester College. And it is a melancholy thought that he should only have become known to the public at large from the exposure, three years ago, of perhaps the most sensational fraud in the history of book-collecting.

As to Wise's stature as a collector, there cannot be two opinions. The libraries formed by Henry Huntington and J. Pierpont Morgan were on a more magnificent scale, as befitted multi-millionaires; others, like those of Sir Leicester Harmsworth or Arnold Klebs, may be in their different fields equally important; but the Ashley Library must be, at the least, one of the half-dozen finest libraries in private hands today, and it is very probably *the* finest. This achievement would be remarkable in a rich man: it is ten times more so in a man who was never rich (in terms of this

---

[1] This obituary article was first published in the *Spectator* of 21 May 1937.

generation's collecting) and who, during the years when the foundations of his collection were being laid, was in hardly more than modest circumstances. The number of items in the Ashley Library which would now fetch over £500 under the hammer runs into hundreds,[1] but those for which their owner paid that sum could probably be counted on the fingers.

Wise was, and indeed seems to have been from his earliest days, a collector of quite uncommon foresight, knowledge, shrewdness, perseverance and acquisitive skill. His tastes must have been formed early, for there are strong echoes of his favourite poets in his own *Verses*, published in 1882 when he was twenty-three years old; and the logical scheme of his great library was planned when most embryo book-collectors are still pottering round David's stall. Wise knew what he wanted and soon learned how to get it. He became a specialist, he realized the value of "original condition," and he published bibliographies—three unusual advantages in the eighteen-nineties. He conducted a bibliographical column in the *Bookman*. He publicized vigorously and acutely. He became the spokesman of the new school of collectors of "moderns"; and with every step up the ladder of prestige his opportunities for advantageous purchase, exchange and sale increased. As *The Times* obituary notice put it, "the financing of the Ashley Library was achieved, partly by skilful selling of duplicates, partly by designing and stocking the libraries of rich collector-aspirants, partly by shrewd copyright speculations"; and anyone who glances through the original Ashley Catalogue (1905–08) may see what strides Wise had already made towards his goal by the turn of the century.

One of the most noticeable tendencies in the book-collecting of the last generation has been the exaltation of

[1] An exaggeration.

"original condition," and although in its more exaggerated forms this has often assumed ridiculous proportions, its essential basis is thoroughly sound. Wise started on re-bound copies, but he was far in advance of most of his contemporaries in that he very soon began to appreciate the importance of the structure of a book—and therefore the necessity of obtaining a copy in the exact state in which it was issued. So that though his library to the end contained a larger number of rebound copies than we nowadays approve (especially among the earlier books), it does show a high proportion of books in original boards, wrappers or cloth; and the very fact that anything else seems unworthy is largely due to the influence of Wise himself.

Wise's influence has been prodigious: and it was exercised in two directions—taste and method. He was the most important member of that group of collectors which from the eighties onwards were concentrating on first editions of the Romantic and Victorian authors, and particularly on the poets. This group included Gosse, Buxton Forman, Axon, Potts, Morgan and Clement Shorter in England, and William Harris Arnold, Halsey, Holden and John H. Wrenn in America. Wise was junior to several of them, but he was the most vigorous and in the end the most successful of them all. He knew W. M. Rossetti; he got to know Browning, Morris, Conrad. And he achieved a foothold at The Pines, which resulted in his being able to purchase from Watts-Dunton, after Swinburne's death, all the poet's remaining manuscripts and printed works which the house contained. He not only acquired books from these authors and their friends, but also made himself an authority on their lives and works; and the fashion for collecting them was firmly cemented by the impressive series of bibliographies in which Wise set out, with a wealth of detail quite new to such type of work, the complete roster of their literary productions.

Wise's dozen bibliographies (ranging from Wordsworth and Coleridge to Conrad), and the eleven massive quarto volumes of the Ashley Library Catalogue,[1] have been a powerful stimulus and advertisement for his type of collecting—complete author-collecting, with marked attention to *Ana*. They are a magnificent monument to the energy and enthusiasm of a great collector with a just and public-spirited pride in his unsurpassed library; and they will always remain valuable works of reference for English poetry and drama from 1650 to 1900, and for sundry novelists as well. But it must be admitted that Wise was not a really good bibliographer. He was full, he was informative, he was on the whole accurate: but he was also often wanting in judgment, often opinionated, and he was not above special pleading where he was determined that his own copy was the right one. And in bibliography, as in any science, the one ultimate necessity is a genuine desire for the truth at all costs. Most of those who have used, and gratefully used, Wise's works for reference have long realized their shortcomings, and have known that where the bibliographer was most dogmatic, there was needed the closest scrutiny of his evidence.

Yet Wise, as time went on, achieved an eminence matched by no living collector. His prestige was such that his conclusions were accepted without question, occasionally in the face of complete confutation by other scholars. His fiat was accorded the finality, the almost papal infallibility, with which it was customarily delivered.

And then suddenly, out of a clear sky, came the exposure as forgeries of a series of fifty-odd "first editions" of various distinguished Victorian authors, all entirely dependent on Wise for their discovery, bibliographical

---

[1] Introductions to these were contributed by Richard Curle, Augustine Birrell, Edmund Gosse, John Drinkwater, E. V. Lucas, A. Edward Newton, R. W. Chapman, D. Nichol Smith, A. W. Pollard, Sir John Squire and Arundell Esdaile.

establishment, provenance, and (most disturbing of all) their market distribution. The best known of these was the famous *Sonnets from the Portuguese* ("Reading, 1847"), which had fetched as much as £250 at auction; and although many of the others were by comparison small fry, all had been treasured by collectors and respected by literary historians for upwards of forty years. The demonstration (until now undisputed) that these books were all printed at one printing-house, at dates ranging up to thirty-eight years later than those on their title-pages, entailed considerable revision in the bibliographies of the authors concerned. It involved the writing-off by innumerable collectors and booksellers of various sums of money, some of them quite substantial. It gave a severe jolt to many people to realize that such a wholesale fraud could still be successfully engineered. But the deeply shocking feature of the whole affair was the fact that Wise, of all men, was intimately mixed up in it. It was almost as if the Bank of England had been caught uttering counterfeit money. Whether Wise was actually responsible for the production of the fakes was not at the time apparent.[1] Opinions differed, though most people found it very difficult to suppose him innocent at least of participation. At any rate it was clear that all the subsequent business of publishing, blurb-writing, advertising, sales promotion, and selling, wholesale and retail, was concentrated in his hands; and it was equally clear that the business had been conducted with extreme skill and marked success.

That Wise should have prostituted bibliography to his own profit was a disgraceful thing; and besides his own great reputation, both the integrity of the science itself and the credit of the trade that lives by it suffered accordingly. But to the initial reactions of anger and dismay was immediately added that of bewilderment. Why should Wise

[1] But see pp. 129 ff.

have risked, for a few thousand pounds, that reputation which he had so long and carefully built up and by which he set such store? Why wreck the credit of a dozen bibliographies for fifty bogus entries? Why invite aspersions on a superlatively great library for the sake of a few cuckoo's eggs?

It was, and it remains, a curious psychological problem. It was at first sight so inexplicable as to constitute a serious obstacle in many people to the admission of Wise's responsibility—they preferred to think he must have been deceived. But he was not deceived: and it would be to deprive a remarkable man of perhaps his most remarkable achievement to pretend any longer that he was. The motives were probably two—the vanity of the rising collector-bibliographer in the discovery of new and exciting first editions; and the need of money. Wise, as not everybody has realized, made a great deal of his money by selling books (in one way or another), and the pamphlets were a very profitable side-line indeed during the heyday of the nineties, when Wise himself was far from affluent. It is to his credit that the profits were put into the Ashley Library rather than devoted to some less worthy end. It is much more to his credit (in the Aristotelian, if not the ethical sense) that the fraud, once embarked on, was carried out with such consummate skill, and on such a heroic scale. The brilliant simplicity of its conception, the typographical appropriateness of the execution, the masterly authority of the establishment, all bespeak the artist: the discretion and efficacy of the marketing and distribution do no less credit to the business man.

Suspicion finally caught up with the "nineteenth-century pamphlets" at a time when the technique of bibliographical expertise had advanced much further than their original (but perhaps not only)[1] begetter could reasonably foresee.

[1] See Part Four of the present book.

They are now being busily collected on their own merits, and it will be disappointing if they are not in future catalogued by the booksellers under Wise's name. At any rate he has the unique honour of two separate niches in the bibliophile's Valhalla—the one beside (though somewhat below) the great Richard Heber, the other next to (and well above) the notorious Ireland: both of them well and truly earned.

TWO BECKFORD COLLECTIONS[1]

WILLIAM BECKFORD, millionaire eccentric, connoisseur, and author of *Vathek*, is not a widely collected author. But over his devotees he seems to exercise a peculiar fascination. Most people have read *Vathek*, which has gone through many editions in the past hundred and twenty-five years, and the first English translation (a sufficiently common book) may be found freely on the shelves of those who collect the outstanding books in English literature. A few discerning readers have discovered the charm of his travel books. Almost nobody has read anything else he wrote; and indeed they cannot be said to have missed much.

This hardly seems a literary career on which to base an author-collection. But in fact Beckford the man is more interesting than any of his books. And the discovery that the travel diaries are frankly, and *Vathek* imaginatively, autobiographical in character brings the appreciative reader back to that extraordinary person, the Abbot of Fonthill, the Sultan of Lansdowne Tower, the Caliph—Beckford himself.

At twenty-one Beckford had the world at his feet. He was handsome and charming, he was extremely and variously accomplished, he had definite talent, he was extravagantly rich. He could have done anything. Unfortunately for him, he had too much imagination—altogether too much. A brilliant Oriental novel was an allowable indulgence for a gentleman. A little normal wildness would have been readily forgiven. Even the passion of his hunting cousin Peter's wife Louisa, which he partly returned, might have been "liquidated" or hushed up. But

[1] This article was first published in the *Colophon*, New Graphic Series, No. I, New York, 1939.

to fall in love with William Courtenay, no mere stableboy but a young man of the highest family, that was beyond forgiveness. Beckford was driven from London into retreat at Fonthill by public outcry in 1784, and out of England by the decree of the family council in the following year, to spend the better part of the next ten years abroad. *Vathek*, published in 1786, fell all but stillborn from the press. *Dreams, Waking Thoughts and Incidents* (1783) had been suppressed before publication. The expected peerage was withheld. And though he lived to build the most sensational house of his generation, to form one of the most remarkable collections of books, manuscripts, pictures, prints, furniture, and objects of vertu in the history of connoisseurship, to marry one of his daughters to a duke, and to attain the age of eighty-four, Beckford never recovered from the effects of the scandal. From being an "original," he became an eccentric. Always a lover of solitude, he became a hermit. By nature and upbringing imperious, he became a tyrant. Yet his most delightful and most finished literary work, *Recollections of an Excursion to the Monasteries of Alcobaça and Batalha*, was written when he was seventy-five years of age.

If the Powderham scandal had allowed *Vathek* to be appreciated when it came out, instead of achieving fame only after Byron's praise; if Beckford had not had to flee the country in the prime of his youth; if he had not lost his devoted and sincerely loved wife, after her second child, in 1786; if he had got the peerage he had been promised—who knows what he might have achieved? Yet if posterity has lost a distinguished public figure and a successful writer, it has at least gained a character as strange and as puzzling as any Byron.

Beckford, as has been already remarked, inspires a special devotion in those who collect him. And our generation has seen half a dozen of these enthusiasts: in England, the late John Hodgkin, most of whose remarkable collection is now in the Bodleian; Mr. Guy Chapman and Lord Esher; and Mr. Michael Sadleir, whose distinguished assemblage is headed by the only known copy, outside public institutions and the family, of *Dreams, Waking Thoughts and Incidents* (1783).[1] In America, there are two fine collections known to me, one in Cambridge, the other in New Haven; and these, in the libraries of Mr. Rowland Burdon-Muller and Mr. James T. Babb respectively, complement each other so prettily that it is instructive to consider them side by side.

Mr. Burdon-Muller, whose summer home is in Switzerland, was first drawn to Beckford by the exile's periodic and lengthy sojourns in his neighbourhood. The author of *Vathek*, like Gibbon before him, is an object of pious curiosity and reverence in the locality, and *Vathek* itself was first published in its original French at Lausanne. What more appropriate than to celebrate his memory with the necessary first editions? Mr. Babb, turning from an energetic collection of moderns, such as Conrad, McFee, and Hemingway, felt inclined, some ten years ago, to try an older author. An admirer of *Vathek*, he decided on Beckford, fancying (in his innocence) that a bibliography so brief promised a quest of manageable length and complexity. He little realized the Caliph's power of fascination, which leads his collectors from one department of *Ana* to another, and has ultimately filled three[2] sizable bookcases and several portfolios in Mr. Babb's library.

The two collections dovetail into each other, and incidentally illustrate two different approaches to an

---

[1] When, some years later, Mr. Sadleir disposed of his Beckfords, this went to Mr. Burdon-Muller. A number of other volumes from his collection were bought by Ray L. Murphy, who bequeathed them to Yale University.

[2] Now more

author-collection. For Mr. Babb is omnivorous, Mr. Burdon-Muller eclectic. Both have nearly all the major first editions, as befits true devotees: but where Mr. Babb will have every issue of every edition of every book, Mr. Burdon-Muller has concentrated more on special copies, and though he might probably buy any edition not in his collection if he found it in fine state, he has not allowed the absence of, say, a scrubby 1819 Paris reprint of *Vathek* to keep him awake at night, rare though it may be.

Mr. Burdon-Muller's Beckfords show a very high level of condition. His first English *Vathek* (1786) in boards, uncut, is fine; his second (1809, and a much rarer book) practically mint. His *Popular Tales of the Germans* (1791) is Beckford's own copy, in full calf by Kalthoeber. *Italy, with Sketches of Spain and Portugal* (1834) and *Monasteries* (1835) are hard to find in fine original state, but here they are. His *Biographical Memoirs of Extraordinary Painters* (1780), Beckford's first book, is in the original marbled boards, calf back, uncut; his first Paris *Vathek* (1787) also uncut; his later editions of both the French and English versions much above the average in condition. His shelf of Beckfordiana—biographical, critical, books from Beckford's library, etc.—is not a long one, but it is fastidiously selected.

Thus far Mr. Burdon-Muller's collection might, in time, be duplicated by another collector of equal taste and discrimination. But it is headed by two brilliant and unique items. The first is Beckford's own set of *Azemia* [1] and *Modern Novel-Writing, or The Elegant Enthusiast*,[2] those entertaining pastiches of the female novelists of the day,

---

[1] *Azemia: a Descriptive and Sentimental Novel. Interspersed with Pieces of Poetry. . . . Dedicated to the Right Honourable Lady Harriet Marlow. To which are added, Criticisms Anticipated*, etc., 2 vols., 1797.

[2] *Modern Novel-Writing, or The Elegant Enthusiast; and Interesting Emotions of Arabella Bloomville. A Rhapsodical Romance: Interspersed with Poetry*, etc., 2 vols., 1796.

and particularly of his half-sister, Mrs. Hervey, which he published under the pen-names of "Jacquetta Agneta Mariana Jenks" and "Lady Harriet Marlow," respectively. The four volumes are bound uniformly in Kalthoeber's most magnificent style, "green morocco gilt elegant"; their pedigree goes directly back, through Lord Rosebery to the Duchess of Hamilton and Brandon, and thus to the author; and the flyleaf of *Modern Novel-Writing* bears an inscription in Beckford's autograph—to himself: "W. B. Presentation copy from the divine authoress."

The other item has an obscurer, less strawberry-leaved, but even more intriguing provenance. This is the celebrated Chavannes copy of the original Lausanne edition of *Vathek* (in a Rivière levant, but uncut and with the original grey wrappers bound in). There is a long inscription in ink all over the title page, and it is this which makes it probably the most interesting copy of *Vathek* in existence today. For many years the obscurity (helped by mistranscription) of the matter, the somewhat unidiomatic French, and the absence of any signature caused the experts to dismiss this inscription as a curiosity, if not a fraud. But more recent research [1] has established with reasonable certainty that it is in the hand of one David Levade and refers to his part in the retranslation of *Vathek* from Henley's English translation into French, for the hastily published Lausanne edition. It is not always realized that *Vathek*, like Gibbon's first book or Wilde's *Salomé* or the works of Mr. Julien Green, was composed in French. It was translated into English by Beckford's tutor, the Rev. Samuel Henley, and first published in English against the exiled author's strict instructions. It is now revealed that Beckford's anxiety to rectify this situation by prompt

[1] See May, *La Jeunesse de Beckford*, passim: *Gazette de Lausanne*, 4 September 1932; John Carter in Bibliographical Society Transactions, March 1937, p. 369; Chapman, *Beckford* (1937), p. 206 and following.

publication of his original was frustrated by the fact that this manuscript was still in Henley's hands, in England. He was therefore obliged to enlist local assistance (from circumstances and lack of time, not from any shortcomings in French, which he spoke like a native) to retranslate from the unauthorized English version, so as to get the Lausanne edition out before the end of the year 1786.

The complementary nature of the Babb collection is startlingly emphasized at this point, because one of its chief treasures is a volume of Beckford's letters to Henley, containing a number written at the very time when the translation, annotation, etc., were going on. Among these is the very one in which Beckford expressly forbade Henley to publish until the French original should be enlarged by the addition of some further *Episodes* (unpublished until 1912) and given a good start over the translation. This fine series of letters derives from the Morrison Collection, having originally been hawked round the London booksellers by Henley until Beckford himself disgustedly bought them back, reputedly for twenty-five pounds.

Beyond these, a number of other letters, and three or four presentation copies (of *Vathek* 1815, both large and small paper, *Monasteries*, etc.), Mr. Babb's collection is less remarkable for individually sensational items than for its astonishing range. Except for the first American,[1] I think he must have every edition of *Vathek* ever printed, going right down to the gutter with a wrappered Newnes issue of the late eighteen-nineties which, in a "Penny Library of Famous Books," included also for good measure *The Anabaptist, a Tale of the 16th Century*, by F. C. Vandervelde. A similar degree of completeness has been achieved in respect of Beckford's other books, as mentioned above, though neither collection includes the two "impossibles," *Dreams, Waking Thoughts and Incidents* (1783)[2] and

[1] Since secured.   [2] See p. 24, footnote 1.

Epitaphs (1823)—extant in four and two copies, respectively. Mr. Babb has preferred, in many cases, an indifferent example to none at all. But now that he is so nearly complete he has begun improving his copies when he can. Yet this activity pales before the enthusiasm of his attack on the dense undergrowth of Beckfordiana, which are truly Beckfordian in their variety, complexity, mystery, and profusion. For besides the ordinary material which derives from any writer who has aroused the curiosity of his contemporaries as well as of posterity, the fantastic edifice which Wyatt built for Beckford at Fonthill has an extensive iconography, not to mention that of his later tower on the hill above Bath—still known in the neighbourhood as Beckford's Folly. Furthermore, Beckford loved making mysteries for future bibliographers to unravel. "If ever the world," he wrote to George Clarke, his bookseller, in 1832, "if ever the world discovers the key of certain anonymous publications, it will find I have not been idle." [1] And Mr. Chapman [2] has listed a number of works attributed to Beckford on one ground or another. Few of these are accepted in the canon; but they are at least entertaining apocrypha, and Mr. Babb has all of them. He even has (God preserve us!) a first edition of the full score of Mozart's *Figaro*. Why? Because Beckford in his old age once said that when he, aged five, was taking music lessons from Mozart, aged nine, the teacher had struck off, as a theme for improvisation by the pupil, the tune of *Non piu andrai*. Q.E.D.

I must resist the temptation to pursue Mr. Babb down any more bypaths, for one last Beckfordian department remains to be mentioned, and one which is well represented in both collections—books from Beckford's library. The Caliph was a prodigious collector, a voracious reader, and a prolific annotator; and in consequence books from his

[1] Chapman, *Bibliography*, p. xix.   [2] *Op. cit.*, p. 81 and following.

library are both commoner and more interesting than usual. Beckford the collector bought the magnificent manuscripts, early printing, and illustrated books appropriate to the period of collecting taste which produced the Roxburghe Club. He went for picked copies, finely bound and richly pedigreed. He had a great deal of taste, a wide knowledge, and a long purse. He led his booksellers a devil of a life.[1] And the Hamilton Palace sales of 1882–1883, in which the main bulk of his library was dispersed, formed one of the high points of the century.

Beckford the reader was no great lover of fiction or poetry, but travels memoirs and general works, both French and English, he bought in abundance and read with attention. He purchased Gibbon's library *en bloc* when he was in Switzerland so as to have something to read, afterwards presenting it to his doctor. He was particular about his binding, much of which was done by Kalthoeber, and he had several special ornaments—notably an outline flower like a cinquefoil and a sort of Maltese cross—by which his books are readily recognizable. These ornaments, which were taken from the Beckford coat of arms, were not only used on the books deemed worthy of half or full leather. They are also regularly found on the very attractive glazed boards of red, green, or blue which he affected for slimmer and more ephemeral volumes. These *cartonnages*, with the edges left untrimmed, are obviously continental in inspiration, and as far as I know they are peculiar to Beckford amongst English collectors of his time.

A great many Beckford books came up in the Rosebery sale in 1933, the earlier Lord Rosebery having been a big buyer at the Hamilton Palace sales; and the majority of those in the two libraries under review derive from this source. Mr. Babb has the only Beckford bookplate I have

[1] A transcript of his letters to George Clarke, from the Bentley library at Upton, is now in the Murphy Collection at Yale.

ever seen, in an 1819 edition of Johnson's *Dictionary*; and also the only two books known to me with his signature—both in schoolbooks, and dated 1771 and 1778 respectively. But Beckford made up for his reticence in the matter of signatures by his constant habit of covering the flyleaves, as he read, with pencil notes. The following, in a volume of the *Quarterly Review*, is typical: "No man equally qualified with Porson to estimate the merits and the vices of Gibbon. Distant and opposite as their habits and manners were; distant and opposite indeed as those of a gentleman and an Hog, they had notwithstanding many points of resemblance. Wit, acuteness, industry, greek, the absence of religion, and a sovereign contempt for dull men who presumed to interfere with them." How judicious, how pungent that is! One looks for the passage which provoked it (Beckford always gives page-references for his notes) and one finds that it is not Beckford's at all, but merely copied from Whitaker's review of the new edition of Gibbon's *Miscellaneous Works*.

So it is with seventy or eighty per cent [1] of Beckford's flyleaf notes: though it is fair to say that he had an excellent eye for the plums, and I know of no better way of perusing a dull book than reading Beckford's extracts of the most amusing stories and pithy phrases, carefully written out at the beginning and end. Sometimes, however, he used flyleaves for more important matter. Mr. Babb has an odd volume of the 1829 Peerage fairly covered with notes for what afterwards became the *Liber Veritatis*, a work which remained in manuscript until 1930, and which Mr. Chapman has neatly described as "Beckford's remedy against the spleen, caused by the elevation to noble rank of persons whom he considered plebeian, in the reigns of George IV and William IV, while he himself was refused a peerage." [2] Then a volume of Pückler Muskau's *Tutti Frutti* (1834)

[1] More.　　[2] *Op. cit.*, p. 76.

contains drafts of passages for the *Monasteries of Alcobaça and Batalha*, which was in process of composition in that year. When Beckford does make a comment on the book he is reading it is usually brief, pertinent, and forcible; and I cannot resist quoting, as a curtain line, the note on the flyleaf of the first edition of *Frankenstein* (also in Mr. Babb's collection). "This is, perhaps," wrote the author of *Vathek*, "the foulest Toadstool that has yet sprung up from the reeking Dunghill of the present Times."

CARROLL ATWOOD WILSON [1]

CARROLL ATWOOD WILSON, who died in 1947, was one of the most distinguished book-collectors of our time. By profession a lawyer, he began serious collecting in 1925 (with a first edition of *The Warden*); and he brought to it a great love of books and their writers, wide reading, a relish for curious and uncanonized merit, an aptitude for bibliographical technique, shrewd judgment and a watchful pertinacity in acquisition, and finally, a resolute thoroughness in his approach to his favourite authors. These, in combination, resulted in a library of an importance quite out of proportion to the outlay involved in its assembly. Wilson had none of the three five-figure Poes, just as his old friend Morris L. Parrish never owned an 1865 *Alice*. But he had something worth the price of ten *Tamerlanes*: a consuming passion directed by a most acute intelligence. And the number of previously unrecorded rarities, unique pieces, precious "association" copies, autograph letters and the like, which adorned particularly his American authors, would make many a millionaire collector green with envy.

Wilson was scholarly without pedantry, tolerant and urbane, a man of sentiment who was also a realist. He loved to unravel a complicated bibliographical problem, to wrestle with the nicest points of chronological priority between one issue and another. But there was no dryness in his virtuosity. His findings in the matter of *Evangeline* for instance, or the "five-star" *Autocrat*, never distracted him from the literary content of the book; and at the end of his exposition of the complexities in some very minor work (just as thorough and carried out with just as much zest) there would often be a deprecatory comment as

[1] This article was first published in *The Times Literary Supplement*, 12 January 1951.

evidence of his unimpaired sense of proportion. He enjoyed a *crux* for its own sake, as a true craftsman; but as a true bibliophile he regarded a "point" as an adornment to, and not something technically separable from, the book in which it might be found.

Wilson's general library was a considerable one. But his collecting activity was concentrated mainly on his favourite nineteenth-century authors, predominantly American; on the first appearances of familiar quotations; and on Gilbert and Sullivan. He was a Savoyard of the Savoyards, leaving almost complete what would have been his most substantial work; a history of the famous partnership written round, and richly illuminated by, the bibliography of the early editions. That it was never completed was due partly to the fact that Wilson was at the same time a perfectionist and a busy man; but more perhaps to the circumstance that he regarded bibliography as the handmaid of scholarship, was himself extremely diffident in publishing even bibliographical material, and always hesitated to plunge into the deep end of the pool of authorship. Indeed, for a man who had so much knowledge that others sought, he published very little. There is the all-too-sparingly annotated catalogue (1945) of his Samuel Butler collection, given to the Chapin Library at Williams College. His catalogue of the Grolier Club's centenary exhibition of Thomas Hardy, published in 1940 by the Colby College Library, is one of the best things of its kind and it consoled many students and collectors for the almost interminable delay in the appearance of Mr. Purdy's long-awaited bibliography.[1] Equally business-like, and fuller, from its nature, of its compiler's loving erudition, was the catalogue of an exhibition of *First Appearance in Print of some Four Hundred Familiar Quotations*, held at Wesleyan University in 1935. Here Wilson brought to full flower that bibliographical homage

[1] Oxford University Press, 1954.

to Bartlett and Burton Stevenson pioneered by Merle Johnson and intensively cultivated by himself, along with Frank Hogan, Mr. David Randall and half a dozen other enthusiasts.

Beyond these there were a few contributions to the Papers of the Bibliographical Society of America, and to other Grolier Club catalogues, as became a devoted and resourceful officer of both these institutions. And there was his collaboration (if that is not too modest a word) in Mr. Richard Curle's *Collecting American First Editions*, a book packed with learning and sanity. But Wilson's preferred method was to open the shelves of his library and the stores of his knowledge to other workers. And this he did with such generous effect that any recent bibliographer in his field whose preface did not contain a tribute to his assistance could almost automatically be suspected of negligence. Yet there inevitably remained in his files much information on which no special call had happened to be made, and it is matter for very real congratulation to those responsible that most of this is now made available in the two handsome volumes under review.[1]

A good deal, but by no means all, of the material in the sections devoted to Hardy and the *Five Centuries of Familiar Quotations* had naturally been used in the publications earlier mentioned. The bibliographical, as distinct from the particular, annotations to the Trollope collection naturally presuppose Sadleir. Messrs Langfeld and Blackburn had drawn upon Wilson's knowledge when preparing their bibliography of Washington Irving. And other findings on individual books had seen the light before. But there is set out here for the first time a mass of bio-bibliographical information on Alcott, Emerson, Hawthorne,

---

[1] Carroll A. Wilson: *Thirteen Author Collections of the Nineteenth Century and Five Centuries of Familiar Quotations*. Edited by Jean C. S. Wilson and David A. Randall. New York: Privately printed for Charles Scribner's Sons. 2 vols. 1950.

Holmes, Irving, Longfellow, Lowell, Melville, Poe, Thoreau, and Whittier such as future students and collectors of any of these authors will neglect at their peril. Much of this derives from the significant presentation inscriptions, and still more from the pertinent autograph letters, the successful assembly of which was perhaps the most remarkable feature of Wilson's collection. He was not content with a glamorous inscription or a fine letter: he sought always something which threw additional light on the writing or the publication of the book. And if the patient skill of the assembly can only be read between the lines by professionals and fellow-collectors, the extraordinary richness of texture in these author-collections is manifest on every page. A single minor entry shall suffice as an example:

The Garden of Kama and other Love Lyrics from India arranged in Verse by Laurence Hope. Third edition.
London 1903.

Inscribed "To Thomas Hardy with sincerest thanks for the hours and hours of pleasure he has given me by his works. Laurence Hope," and with Max Gate book-label.

Enclosed are two cards and a t.l.s., signed with the author's real name, Violet Nicolson, to Hardy, a long letter from her solicitor, with full explanation of her suicide and the spiritual reason therefor, and an a.l.s. from Gosse to Hardy, revealing that on the very day she died he and Hardy were discussing her poems.

Also inserted, the original draft of MS. of Hardy's obituary notice of Laurence Hope for *The Athenaeum*, Oct. 29, 1904, some 300 words, much corrected, a beautifully written tribute to a poet and poetry which he clearly valued very highly. This tribute appears without signature, and it is not generally known that Hardy wrote it. I have noted a few slight differences between this MS. and the final form, a type-written copy of which accompanies this.

With these also is the a.l.s., 2pp., signed "Thomas Hardy," dated Max Gate, Oct. 23, 1904, to the editor of *The Athenaeum*, showing that Hardy to a certain extent solicited the opportunity.

This entry also shows how nearly Wilson approximated to that Utopian ideal of an author-collector once delineated by his friend, Mr. John T. Winterich (in *New Paths in Book-Collecting*, 1934). He was not content with all the variants, if any, of the original edition; he would have magazine appearances of individual pieces, serial printings of full-length works (the magazine texts of Hardy, for instance, make an astonishing show), any later editions with new matter, first appearances in book form, first separate editions, theatre programmes—everything by, with or from his author. And this was no mere omnivorous accumulation: for their collector was a shrewd textual critic, and his comparisons of one printing with another provided matter for many an elucidatory comment. The result was a group of author-collections each one of which, in its cumulative and associative effect, was infinitely more important than the sum of its component parts. It is therefore most welcome news that, except for Holmes, whose importance is half literary and half medical, the booksellers who purchased the library have succeeded in keeping the American collections intact: the Emersons and Whittiers having been bought for Duke University and Swarthmore College respectively, and all the remainder by a private collector [1] who intends, it is understood, to bequeath them to the University of Virginia.

The catalogue now published has been edited, from Wilson's own copious descriptions, by his widow and one of his closest friends. The formula of description used for the entries is of the simplest, unless the item is un-described elsewhere; and only variant bindings are recorded, since the reader is expected to know what the normal original binding was. The arrangement of the author-sections (except for Trollope) is chronological. But there is no serial numeration, which is always helpful

[1] Mr. C. Waller Barrett, of New York.

for reference to a work of this kind. Fidelity to Wilson's *ipsissima verba* has retained some careless phraseology, a few sweeping statements and some other details which he himself would probably have excised for the printer. But it has preserved much characteristic comment and personal flavour which also might not have survived his own editing, so that the gain is much greater than the loss. What the editors have not done—something which all except the most expert reader would have welcomed—is to expand Wilson's almost shorthand allusions to bibliographies and other specialized reference books. A man moving among familiar tools may well write, on his own catalogue sheets, "see Brussel," or "Maier Catalogue," or "not in Foley," or "the bibliography is incorrect." But it is not fair either to him or to the reader to leave these *sigla* completely unidentified, when a few footnotes would have sufficed for their clarification. As a result, many notes which could have been plain are puzzling, and a few (e.g., that to Alcott's *Proverb Stories*, 1882) are positively cryptic. There are other notes (e.g., to Hardy's *Three Notable Stories*, 1890, or Hawthorne's *The Celestial Railroad*, 1843) in which Wilson had failed to make himself clear in a piece of bibliographical exposition or deduction: whether, again, from over-familiarity with the details, from the absence of final polishing, or from plain human fallibility. It was presumably piety and not negligence on the part of the editors to leave these obscurities intact: but many readers will consider the piety mistaken, and will think that if such notes could not be mended, they were better omitted.

Yet these blemishes are of minor consequence in a work of nearly 900 pages which describes scores of pieces hitherto unrecorded in print, which provides a series of absolutely indispensable supplements to the bibliographies of the authors included in it, which gives the full text of hundreds of their letters, and which consistently illuminates their lives as well as their printed works. Wilson presumed a knowledge of the rudiments, and even if his editors had done a little more editing it would still not be a book for bibliographical tyros. It is a tour, conducted with an affable mastery of the technical equipment, round one of the great collections of our generation. There are no pictures, there is no pomp and circumstance (except the affectation of unopened leaves), there is no vanity, and there are no superlatives of rarity without ample—often more than ample—evidence. Every page catches Wilson's accent and something of his own exhilarating personality; and if those who frequented the library during his lifetime recall that the talk there was commonly sweetened with something printers do not provide—namely, a glass or two of bourbon whisky, they will perhaps console themselves with the reflection that this congenial liquid is not unknown in the university to which so large a part of Wilson's library is ultimately destined. He himself was a Yankee, and most of the American authors he collected were Northerners. But if, when that time comes, the North still needs such ambassadors as these in Charlottesville, their credentials will already be on record.

MICHAEL SADLEIR[1]

It is given to few book-collectors to exert a decisive influence on the technique as well as on the taste of their age. When the history of bibliophily comes to be written, obeisance will justly be made, in the chapter dealing with the nineteenth century, to the memory of, for example, the third Duke of Roxburghe, of Frederick Locker and of Thomas J. Wise. And this will be owing less to the importance of the libraries they formed—for those of Lord Spencer, Christie Miller, Lenox, Huth, Hoe and others were greater—than to the effect of their collecting philosophy on their contemporaries and successors. It is one thing, and a very fine thing, to assemble a great collection in the classic tradition or in the prevailing manner. It is another thing, and a much rarer one, to change the whole climate of book-collecting.

If a contemporary Beckford were writing another *Dialogue in the Shades*, the ghosts of J. P. Morgan, Henry Huntington and Bernard Quaritch might be expected to maintain (like Sir Thomas Browne) that, by the arrival on the scene of the present generation, the great mutations of the world were over: that to glean where the giants had reaped could no doubt instruct and stimulate—but would still be no more than gleaning. The spokesman for the moderns could deploy in rebuttal two powerful arguments. In defence he could insist, and it would be true, that such contemporary collectors as Dr. Bodmer, Mr. Houghton, Mr. Rosenwald or Mr. Lilly—to name but a handful—could have held their own with the biggest guns of the past in the broadest fields of bibliophily. And in counterattack, he could point with justifiable pride to the wider

[1] This article was first published in *The Times Literary Supplement*, 13 April 1951.

horizons and deeper penetrations of contemporary taste, the fastidious precision and bibliographically expert direction of contemporary technique. To Bernard Quaritch in particular he would rehearse the names of G. D. Hobson, A. W. Evans and Lathrop Harper, of E. P. Goldschmidt and Mr. F. S. Ferguson, as evidence that those professionals on whom the amateurs must always depend have more than maintained his own loyalty to the scholarly tradition of William Pickering and Henry Stevens. In deference to the great collectors he would perhaps refrain from pressing the claims of their more obvious descendants, and would concentrate on an exposition of those striking developments in the whole texture of bibliophily which have characterized the past three decades—proving, perhaps, once again that the humanities flourish rather than wilt during times of tumult and violence.

If our spokesman decided to limit his area of counter-attack, he might well choose, as favourable ground for illustrating his argument, the collecting of nineteenth-century books in general, but of fiction in particular. And he would certainly cite, among its principal strategists, the names of Morris L. Parrish, Carroll A. Wilson, and Mr. Michael Sadleir. The two Americans, though very recently dead, are already (one doubts not) on familiar terms with their illustrious predecessors, in that book-lined portico on the slopes of Parnassus where Aurispa and Archbishop Parker, Grenville and Renouard take their ease. But Mr. Sadleir, as the handsome quarto volumes before us bear witness, is still very much with us; and his two friends would have been the first to proclaim that this catalogue [1] crowns a body of work unmatched for its influence on Anglo-American book-collecting in our time.

When discussing the bibliophilic invasion of Victorian

[1] Michael Sadleir. *XIX Century Fiction.* A Bibliographical Record based on his own collection. In Two Volumes. London, Constable & Co.; Los Angeles, University of California Press. 1951.

literature in the Sandars Lectures for 1947, I was careful to point out that it was no mere fashion but rather "the collector's expression of a much wider development in public taste." I considered, on the other hand, that "it would be as idle as unjust to deny full weight to the influence of those collectors and bibliographers who had pioneered the Victorian revival and now [i.e., in the 1930s] helped to chart its course." After mentioning Parrish and Wilson, A. E. Newton, Sir Hugh Walpole and Lord Esher, among those who gave the movement added momentum, I concluded that

to one man in particular, Mr. Michael Sadleir, the collecting of Victorian fiction owed not only momentum but direction and breadth. In his bibliography of Trollope, in his *Publishers' Binding Styles*, in his studies of the fiction reprint series, even as early as his pioneer *Excursions in Victorian Bibliography* (1922), there was revealed an acute perception of that fourth dimension in collecting technique; the publishing background of the books collected . . . [and] it was the good fortune of those who began to collect the Victorians in the thirties that this method of approach preceded, instead of following, popular attention. Mr. Sadleir's researches into the general problem of comparative rarity, his attention to book-structure and distribution methods, his analysis of the bibliography of any given book in the light of its publisher's as well as its author's temperament and practice, set a wholly new standard for collectors as well as bibliographers. Being himself an author and a publisher as well as a collector and bibliographer, he understood very well how much the two latter have to learn about the two former. And his influence on both sides of the Atlantic has been such that the collecting of modern books in general, as well as his favourite Victorian novelists, has since been approached with a reasoned intelligence, a regard for causes as well as effects, by many collectors who would twenty years ago have considered as pedantic if not pretentious many things they now do as a matter of course. This was a development in method of profound and salutary importance.

It must be remembered that the measured verdict of one

Sandars Reader in Bibliography on another was also the tribute of a disciple; for it was Mr. Sadleir who, twenty years ago, commissioned my first book, and that book was avowedly a footnote, if a considerably swollen footnote, to one of his own. But it would be difficult to find anyone capable of a considered appraisal of Mr. Sadleir's work who was not also heavily indebted to it himself. This one, therefore, may perhaps be allowed to stand for the time being: and it is certainly apposite to the present context, for the special qualities singled out for comment are exhibited in ample, unhurried, and pre-eminent form in *XIX Century Fiction*.

This catalogue is introduced by what Mr. Sadleir has called "Passages from the Autobiography of a Bibliomaniac"; a preliminary version of which was delivered as a paper to the Bibliographical Society during the author's presidential year. In this instructive document Mr. Sadleir has not only traced the development of his career as a book-collector, but has also allowed us a number of significant glimpses of the principles which have guided, and the seeming accidents which have helped to shape, that career.

It was his early concentration on Trollope, he tells us, which taught him "to love the Victorian novel *as a material thing*." The earliest published fruits of this continuing love were the *Excursions in Victorian Bibliography* of 1922; but *Trollope, a Commentary* (1927) and *Trollope, a Bibliography* (1928) represented "the first full-length application of a principle which had from the beginning influenced my book-collecting policy and was to become an integral part of it. I have never undertaken the intensive collection of any author or movement without the intention of ultimately writing the material collected into biography, bibliography, or fiction." The original Trollope collection, after an improving sojourn in M. L. Parrish's library, is now at Princeton. It will never be surpassed for quality.[1] Nor, though Mr. Sadleir offers half a dozen additions and corrections in the present catalogue, is the bibliography based on it likely to be dethroned from its generally accepted position as the model treatment of a nineteenth-century author. As for fiction, readers who have been curious about the wealth of local colour in *Fanny by Gaslight* or *Forlorn Sunset* will find a number of intriguingly titled specimens of the source material in the second volume of the present catalogue.

Mr. Sadleir's use of the word *policy* will not have passed unnoticed. His approach to book-collecting has from the beginning been thoughtful without solemnity, carefully planned but flexible, adventurous yet proof against the attraction of peripheral blind alleys. He has always been ready to expand in a fresh direction; but the graft is required to be congenial to the main stem, the additions to contribute something functional, not merely decorative, to the main design. This underlying, sometimes almost sub-conscious, conception of the potentialities for fruitful development of his broad theme has kept Mr. Sadleir perpetually alert, uncannily sensitive to half-veiled opportunities, magnetically attractive as a collector to hauls of unsifted ore from all sorts of unexpected quarries. The "accidents" of bulk acquisition, which seem in his narrative to have shaped the development of his library, were not accidents in the true sense; for things only fall into a man's lap if he has contrived to have his lap in the right place. Mr. Sadleir's purchases of the Syston Park Gothic novels, of Arthur Hutchinson's huge fiction hoard, of the Molineaux yellow-backs, of the Bentley three-deckers; his seizure of the opportunity offered by the dispersal of the fabulous Mount Bellew Library, his clean sweep of the "Silver Fork" novels in the Rhiwlas Library—these were not accidents,

---

[1] Unless by Mr. Sadleir himself.

nor even inspired impulses: they were the bold, imaginative, but confident tactics of a collector who is master of his own strategy.

It is matter for regret that the great collection of Gothic novels left Mr. Sadleir's shelves (for the University of Virginia) before he could apply to it on any considerable scale his principle of publishing the digested results of this bibliophile enthusiasm. For no other annotation to what would be a most valuable catalogue can be expected to match his unique blend of literary sensibility, bibliographical knowledge and collecting experience. Yet, after all, nineteenth-century fiction has been his main field, and one so pre-eminently his that the publication of this long-awaited survey is *ipso facto* an event of major consequence to the bibliographical and book-collecting communities. Indeed, its range of interest goes far beyond these restricted circles: for these two volumes offer a documented and richly annotated survey not only of fiction-writing in an immensely various and prolific period, but also of book-structure, publishing practice, distribution technique, author-publisher relationships, and (last but not least) the reading habits of the age.

The first and fatter volume contains, in one author-alphabet, full descriptions of the first (and certain subsequent) editions of all the authors in the collection, followed by an appendix discussing comparative scarcities among the works of the major novelists, thirty-two pages of illustrations, and an index of titles. Many of the authors are given a general preliminary note; the notes to individual books vary with their complexity rather than with their literary importance; and the condition of the copy is scrupulously assessed. There are no signature-collations, but the descriptive formula is generally adequate to the material. Bindings are treated with the fullness which Mr. Sadleir himself has taught us that they deserve. He is admirably precise about half-titles and blank leaves. He records inserted advertisements where they are present, without dogmatism as to whether they need be; though there are perhaps half a dozen examples where one cannot tell whether the advertisements are inserts or integral to the collation. The half-tone plates are mostly very clear, though photographs can hardly ever do justice to fine boarded books; and while the sequence gives us a bird's-eye view of a century's evolution in publishers' binding styles, individual plates (such as that showing the four bindings of *The House by the Church Yard*) will be invaluable to amateurs of variants. The last three plates show 24 specimen types of binding-cloth. Both in the captions to these and among the descriptions of bindings in the catalogue (which are never, surprisingly, keyed to the appropriate specimen by a cross-reference) Mr. Sadleir has expanded and refined his system of nomenclature for cloth-fabrics to a point which should encourage other bibliographers to accept it as standard.[1] He has obviously given equally careful thought to the more intractable problem of describing accurately the colour of a publisher's cloth binding: often a matter of importance to bibliographers and collectors, and as yet hopelessly lacking in any uniformity of usage beyond the most primary of tints. It will probably remain impossible to systematize such descriptions, unless we are prepared to adopt the British Colour Council's chart, make it a compulsory plate in every bibliography and catalogue, and key all descriptions to it by number. But Mr. Sadleir has substantially enlarged on the normal vocabulary, so that his pages are pleasingly dotted with moss-greens, loam-browns, rose-madders, Cambridge blues and the like.

One criticism may be made of the presentation of this catalogue as a whole. It would surely have given us a

[1] But see p. 175, footnote 4.

clearer and more informative picture of an author's development if his or her books had been set out chronologically, rather than alphabetically by titles (the searcher after a particular book can always refer to the title index). Apart from the generally disruptive effect of the alphabet on the literary sequence of an author's *œuvre*, this arrangement deprives us also of an easy view of his progress from one publisher to another, or from one kind of physical form to another—both of them matters in which we have learned, at Mr. Sadleir's own feet, to take an intelligent interest. And even to those who care nothing for such things, it is disconcerting to find, for instance, Maria Edgeworth's *Continuation of Early Lessons* (1814) immediately preceding *Early Lessons* (1801) itself, Seton Merriman's first book the last of the 21 listed, or a note (attached to *Ariadne*, 1877) on Ouida's change from Chapman and Hall to Chatto and Windus when the only book yet described for us was published twenty years later by Fisher Unwin. If this inconvenience is no less severe in Section II, the Yellow-Back Collection, it is even more severe in Section III, wherein is described Mr. Sadleir's incomparable assembly of "Novelist's Libraries," "Standard Libraries," "The Parlour Library" and other cloth, or cloth and boarded, fiction series. For these last, especially, need to be studied as the successive, constantly evolving, and often frankly imitative efforts of the publishing trade to develop a market for well-produced, readable, cheap fiction. And it is correspondingly inconvenient to have to follow our guide backwards and forwards, just because Harrison and Mudford and Whittingham follow Blackwood and Chapman and Hall in the alphabet.

Yet the wealth of interest which this section holds is such that one reader at least would have devoured every word of it, quite cheerfully, standing on his head. Only professionals, perhaps, and an experienced few among Mr.

Sadleir's fellow-collectors, can appreciate to the full the astonishing feat of the mere assembling of these long runs of unregarded, largely ephemeral, fiction series; in their original bindings, and almost all in what the *cognoscenti* call "Jennings condition," after that most fastidious of collectors, to whom this catalogue is dedicated. But anyone interested in books and reading, of any period, must be enthralled by Mr. Sadleir's full, discerning, carefully documented commentary on the development of this venturesome expansion of the range of publishing. The essays on Bentley, Colburn, the Parlour Library (that revolutionary experiment of a Belfast printer), the Novel Newspaper, and the Library of Romance remain particularly in the memory, as do Mr. Sadleir's accounts (written with all the feeling of a practising publisher) of the periodic attempts to break the stranglehold of the circulating libraries on the new fiction market.

The second volume has its own plates, 16 pages of them. And if the eye pauses respectfully on the workmanlike bindings of Bentley's Standard Novels or the Parlour Novelist, it is the yellow-backs which undoubtedly steal the show. This is a class of book which Mr. Sadleir has rescued, almost single-handed, from contemptuous oblivion: his pioneer essay in *New Paths in Book-Collecting* received a very chilly welcome from the pundits in 1934, and it is fair to say that the yellow-backs of the decadence (say, 1880–1900) seldom deserve anything much warmer today. But, even without their essential colour, Mr. Sadleir's chosen specimens from the earlier years (and the first authentic examples date from 1853) support to the full his considered and studiously moderate estimate of their physical merits and interest of content. It is seldom realized, for instance, that the yellow-back was the original medium for 95 per cent of detective fiction during the incunabular decade between Poe and *The Moonstone*. Nor was this by any means the only material of historical and literary significance to make its first bow to the public in this rowdy dress. To anyone whose memory of yellow-backs is bounded by a shelf of grubby, tattered, routine volumes dating from about 1890, the sight of a bookcase full of the gay, individually designed, highly glazed eighteen-pennyworths which tempted the railway traveller of 1860 is a revelation. The trouble is that such a sight is almost impossible to recreate today (did we not hear recently that even the earlier Penguins were already unobtainable?). But if Mr. Sadleir has almost cornered the originals he has managed to communicate a surprisingly vivid character-sketch in *XIX Century Fiction*.

At this point it is perhaps useful to remind ourselves, by a glance at the contents of the main alphabet, that to identify Mr. Sadleir with the Victorians is to overlook his equally perspicacious (and today even more suggestive) preoccupation with the Regency novelists. This indeed could never have been forgotten by those many good judges who consider *Edward and Rosina* his own best (as it was his least commercially successful) book. But even they might be surprised at the impressive showing made here by the fictions (Mr. Sadleir's word) published between 1800 and 1837, especially when it is observed that though Michael Scott is 100 per cent present, there is nothing by Sir Walter. Taking the century as a whole, the most notable author-collections described here are probably the following: the Banims, Miss Braddon, the Brontë sisters, Bulwer, Carleton, Wilkie Collins, Disraeli, Maria Edgeworth, Mrs. Gaskell, Mrs. Gore, Henry Kingsley, Le Fanu, Marryat, Maturin, Meredith, Merriman, Lady Morgan, Morier, Mrs. Oliphant, Ouida, Mayne Reid, the Trollope family (other than Anthony) and Mrs. Henry Wood. Specialists could cite other libraries, though probably no private library, which could challenge Mr. Sadleir on the last two-thirds of the century, as represented here, in first edition *and* in immaculate original state: but they would have a much harder time with the first third. And a score of minor novelists of the period have not even been mentioned.

It remains to observe that Mr. Sadleir, who has a distaste for part-issues in general, has assembled a collection of Dickens first editions in cloth which could not be equalled for condition in ten years' search (they are far rarer than equally good sets of parts); that his distaste for Thackeray in particular has not prevented him from acquiring the only two Thackeray three-deckers; and that he has chosen to include, in a predominantly British list, first English editions of works by Hawthorne, Melville, Tolstoy, Turgenev, Twain and Zola. It must be noted that half a dozen items by well-known authors are here described in print for the first time; that certain "obvious" first editions by well-represented authors are absent—e.g., *Mary Barton*, *Workers in the Dawn*, *Lady Audley's Secret* and the two rarest Conan Doyles; and that a number of towering books are present in spectacularly fine original state—e.g., *The Woman in White* (of which the English edition, *pace* Mr. Sadleir's note, probably preceded the American), *The Whale* (i.e., *Moby Dick*), perhaps the most dazzling three-decker of the entire century, and *Wuthering Heights*, of which Mr. Sadleir's copy may be set down without equivocation as the finest in existence.

Finally a word must be said about the appendix on "Comparative Scarcities." Mr. Sadleir's scrupulous respect for the epithet "rare" may be judged by his omission to apply it, in the catalogue, to such notorious rarities as *The Heir of Redclyffe*, *An Irish Cousin* (the first novel of Somerville and Ross), or (in really fine state) *Handy Andy* by Samuel Lover—of the first, Mr. Sadleir's copy is the only one to have appeared in the market in a quarter of a century and of the second his is one of only two to have been recorded during the same period. His application to the works of 26 authors, therefore, of the principles of comparative scarcity first evolved in his bibliography of Trollope, will be welcomed with open arms by collectors and booksellers alike; and the latter might well consider these ten pages alone to be worth the price of the whole book. A few people may suppose themselves qualified to dissent from some of the conclusions reached by Mr. Sadleir after collation (he tells us) with the experience of a group of likeminded experts—among them, no doubt, Mr. Dudley Massey, whose assistance in the whole work is warmly acknowledged in the preface. But they will be very few, and they will be properly diffident. The present reviewer would be prepared to submit that certain schedules —e.g. for Hardy—disregard issue-points; to argue some isolated titles—maintaining, e.g., that *Barchester Towers* is rarer than *The Three Clerks*, Le Fanu's *Ghost Stories* than his *All in the Dark*, *The Egoist* than *Beauchamp's Career*; and to suggest that Mr. Sadleir's analysis of George Eliot scarcities takes insufficient account of the Blackwood records, either in the matter of printing-numbers of the later novels or of the purchases of the circulating libraries. But for the great majority of the books concerned these estimates will be accepted, and rightly, as the nearest thing to certitude that we are likely to get—and that is a great deal more than any authority has even thought of trying to achieve for a comparable body of books in any other period whatsoever. That this is no more than a by-product of Mr. Sadleir's work in his chosen field is a measure of the stature and achievement of the most accomplished book-collector of our time.

WILMARTH S. LEWIS

MR. WILMARTH LEWIS is an example of that very rare phenomenon, an unabashed fanatic with a lively sense of humour. Awed observers of his single-minded quest have from time to time predicted that he would end up in a padded library under the delusion that he *was* Horace Walpole; but they overlooked his remarkable capacity for making fun of his own enthusiasms. In the reminiscences now before us [1] Mr. Lewis proves himself as gaily skilful a writer as he is collector, and the result is a conspicuously attractive book.

The fact that Mr. Lewis is constitutionally incapable of being earnest does not mean that he is not serious. On the contrary, his seriousness of purpose, his pertinacity, his patience, his machiavellian combinations, his delicacy of touch have put him among the small handful of really masterly strategists in the book-collecting field of today. And to these qualities has been added that sixth sense which leaves the mere tactician floundering in the rear— the ability to smell, from the next room, or even from the next county, some piece of Walpoliana which the owner did not even know was there. The physical result of twenty-five years' intense concentration is the *Museum Arbuteanum* at Farmington, Connecticut: a re-creation of Strawberry Hill at once scholarly and affectionate; an internationally recognized *enclave* of the great library at Yale; a beehive of eighteenth-century studies; a vindication of connoisseurship against the charge of dilettantism; the *ne plus ultra* of author-collecting—in short, a nonpareil on the literary as well as the bibliophile horizon.

[1] *Collector's Progress.* London, Constable & Co.: New York, Alfred A. Knopf. 1952. This article was first published in *The Times Literary Supplement*, 9 May 1952.

For Mr. Lewis's collecting has been a means to an end. "The collector's work," he has said, "is only partly done when he has formed his collection. Unless it is used it is like bric-a-brac in a cabinet." To him, therefore, the great "Gothic lanthorn" from Strawberry Hill, the door from Walpole's house in Berkeley Square, the silhouette portrait of the Duchess of Grafton with his manuscript caption, and a copy of Kirgate's forgery of Gray's *Odes*, are all part of the rich, leisurely, elaborate tapestry of which the main threads are formed by Horace Walpole's writings and—pre-eminently—his correspondence. Of the Yale Edition of that enormous correspondence, with its even more enormous complement of annotation, Mr. Lewis is the architect, sponsor and editor-in-chief. Fourteen stout quarto volumes have so far appeared.[1] The fiftieth is scheduled for publication on his seventieth birthday, in 1965. The first-fruits of this majestic enterprise were saluted in *The Times Literary Supplement* with the prophecy that "if the event is equal to its promise, it may well eclipse the Variorum Shakespeare as the greatest achievement of editorial scholarship in the United States." In spite of the competition since offered by Yale's acquisition of the Boswell Papers, Mr. Lewis and his colleagues show no signs of belying this ambitious forecast.

Collector's Progress is, to be sure, almost entirely concerned with Walpole—books and manuscripts by and belonging to him, letters written by and to him, prints, drawings and relics of Strawberry Hill and products of its press, portraits, pamphlets and *Ana* of every kind bearing directly or indirectly on Walpole's personality, friendships, dislikes, interests—his period as a whole. But Mr. Lewis has woven all this into the story of his collecting life with such artistry that Mann and Cole and Lady Ossory appear in the same perspective, to his readers, as Paget Toynbee,

[1] As of 1952.

Professor Tinker and the two commissionaires in the British Museum's Department of Manuscripts. It is a story which will entertain and instruct many others besides collectors and eighteenth-century specialists: not only by its wealth of anecdote and its easy, often racy, style, but by the singularly agreeable impression which it consistently conveys both of its author's dedicated humanism and of the pleasing warmth generated in all sorts and kinds of people by exposure to Mr. Lewis's enthusiastic ingenuity and persistence as a collector.

The account of his development from tyro to master of this subtle craft provides the framework of the book. It is enlivened with some capital character-sketches—among them Seymour de Ricci, A. W. Evans, Richard Bentley of Upton (a particularly good set-piece) and a London book-seller called Mr. X whom few collectors or professionals over thirty will have much difficulty in identifying. There are some splendid bits of patient detective work, for which the prize must undoubtedly go to "The Case of the Dismembered *Theatre of Geo. III*," solved in co-operation with Messrs Pickering and Chatto. There are successful hunches, and disappointments, extraordinary coincidences and happy examples of serendipity. Walpole letters turn up in Australia and Peru. There are glimpses, but no more, of the laborious spadework of research, the patient tracing of a lost item through the labyrinth of old sale catalogues, its possible owner through Burke or Debrett: that silent, unseen, essential preparation for the dazzling, the seemingly effortless *coup*. There is, indeed, plenty to engross even the reader who supposes Horace Walpole to be the author of *Rogue Herries*.

For Mr. Lewis's fellow-collectors, and for the book-sellers whom he so warmly esteems, there is also, of course, much more. Some of it has to be read between the lines: partly because Mr. Lewis recounts most of his successes with becoming modesty, partly because *virtuosi* still in active practice do not care to photograph their own sleights of hand. But behind the sometimes deceptively casual air, behind the elliptical treatment of certain phases in a transaction, the discerning will recognize a collecting technique of a very high order. In a business deal we perceive that Mr. Lewis can be thoroughly businesslike. But much of the most important material now at Farmington lay in places where to be businesslike would have been fatal. Stately homes, backwoods squirearchy, sturdy independents, institutional libraries—the approach to these called for the utmost in delicacy, discretion and address. It is abundantly clear that Mr. Lewis is a serious loss to his country's diplomatic service.

Perhaps his most impressive achievement in the purely technical sphere can hardly be appreciated by the layman. It is that, in spite of being fairly rich and having been known for twenty years as the keenest Horace Walpole collector in the world, he has managed to avoid putting prices up against himself. To be a magnet is very well; to be a target can be expensive. There must have been many occasions when more than one bookseller reckoned that here was something Mr. Lewis had simply got to have, and resolved to outbid his neighbour for the privilege of selling it to him. There may even have been times when a dealer not favoured with a commission from Farmington thought to teach Mr. Lewis and his agent a lesson. Only a combination of resolution and finesse with the power to attract and retain the trade's goodwill could have kept the tortuous course between the Scylla of an extortionate price and the Charybdis of a missed opportunity. Mr. Lewis, with a studiously *dégagé* hand on the tiller and his cap at the jauntiest of angles, has made such a course seem like a straight line. The measure of his mastery of the market may be taken by comparing his account of the sort of opposition he encountered at the Beverly Chew sale in 1924 with his practically clean sweep of the Walpoliana in the Spoor sale of 1939 and his performance at the Waller sale in 1947. Here, of the forty-four Walpole lots, he "was able to get all but two," though he does not tell us that not all of these fell to his agent's bids.

Part of Mr. Lewis's increasing immunity from competition has been due, it is true, to the forbearance of other collectors, most of whom have by now tacitly accepted the proposition that anything remotely Walpolian belongs by right at Farmington. Even if bibliophiles as a class are not as curmudgeonly as their critics sometimes suppose, it is still eloquent testimony to Mr. Lewis's international reputation that his natural rivals, instead of swooping on some enviable piece and thus winning a trick from the maestro, tend rather to withdraw in his favour—and even to keep a spare eye open in his interest. Nor, indeed, have certain university and public libraries been able to resist the magnetic authority of the *Museum Arbuteanum*, exercised as it is with Mr. Lewis's polished urbanity. *Quid plura?*

LORD ROTHSCHILD

PERHAPS not an innovation but certainly a distinct and notable change in bibliophilic strategy emerged as the [1930s] wore on: specialization in a period. The textbook example of this rewarding compromise between the general and the particular is probably Lord Rothschild's eighteenth-century library. Here, in little more than a dozen years' collecting, has been demonstrated that the choice of a target of a size strictly consonant not only with the available attention and means but, more significantly, with the expectable availability of material, is of fundamental importance in the planning of any collection. In the tactical area, the result also demonstrates that just as there is a right size for all things, so is there a right time. . . . Lord Rothschild was able to take advantage of that violent reaction of the majority against eighteenth-century books which followed the boom of the twenties. For some years at any rate competition would be limited; a keen buyer in a temporarily unfashionable department would get the offers; and a resolute beginning might secure foundations which ten years later would need twenty years of patient laying.

So wrote the author of *Taste and Technique in Book Collecting*,[1] published in 1948: the year in which, as we now learn, Lord Rothschild decided to conclude his all-out attack on the eighteenth century. There have been subsequent additions, most notably among the fine bindings, which are given a separate section in this catalogue. But to all intents and purposes the Rothschild library, which is here described[2] with a scholarship and an elegance worthy of its contents, was assembled in little more than a dozen years.

The foreword is all too laconic. Those of its readers who

[1] I am sorry to keep quoting myself: but there it is.
[2] *The Rothschild Library*. A Catalogue of the Collection of Eighteenth-Century Printed Books and Manuscripts Formed by Lord Rothschild. In Two Volumes. Privately Printed at the University Press, Cambridge. 1954. This article was first published in *The Times Literary Supplement*, 18 March 1955.

remember, for instance, the series of introductions to the Ashley Catalogue, written by a number of experts who assumed without apparent disrelish the role of caryatids to Wise's temple of fame,[1] will no doubt understand Lord Rothschild's addiction to the proposition that good wine needs no bush. Yet unless the erstwhile Sandars Reader in Bibliography was wholly in error in attributing a definite purpose and pattern to the formation of this distinguished and widely reputed collection, there will be many appreciative users of a valuable reference book who would have welcomed some account of the assembly of its contents. The *memorabilia* of thoughtful collectors—and it is unfortunately clear that Lord Rothschild would be writing in the past, not the present, tense—are not only of importance to the historian of bibliophilic taste and technique: they can also be of constructive interest to contemporary collectors.

Lord Rothschild recalls that his active involvement with English literature was imposed upon the budding scientist by the requirements of a pass degree at Cambridge; and that the original direction of his enthusiasm into bibliophilic channels was due to Mr. George Rylands of King's. He does not specifically confirm the tradition that his concentration on the eighteenth century in general and Jonathan Swift in particular derived from a then consuming admiration for the *Meditation on a Broomstick*; nor does he tell us a word of what went on between his first innocent purchases in the early thirties and the date at which he began (methodically—and appropriately—with the circulation of *Proposals*) to plan his catalogue of the completed collection.

He pays generous tribute to the guiding hand of Mr. John Hayward, and among his further acknowledgments the knowledgeable will not be surprised to find in the place

See p. 18, footnote.

of honour Messrs R. W. Chapman, Herbert Davis, Philip
Gaskell and A. N. L. Munby. The list of "distinguished
experts" to whom the *Proposals* were submitted for comment includes, besides eighteen names which will be toler-
ably familiar, one significant one which may not be; it is
that of Mr. R. Lewis, cataloguer-in-chief to the firm of
West End booksellers who probably supplied (the auction
rooms aside) more of the books and manuscripts here
described than the rest of the antiquarian trade of London
and New York put together.

The catalogue, we learn with respect, is largely the work
of Miss N. M. Shawyer. It comprises, after the usual pre-
liminaries, an author alphabet (including a few owners of
books acquired for their owner-interest); sections devoted
to the Baskerville, Foulis and Strawberry Hill presses;
sections describing English, Scottish, and Irish bindings
of the eighteenth century; some appendixes for special
collections (e.g., the Poley pamphlets, the Rolle plays);
and a series of indexes. There are sixty plates (excellent
photographs, excellently reproduced), with an ingenious
method of indicating reduction. The formulae of transcription and description are clear, sufficient and unpedantic.
The typographical articulation of the entries has a family
affinity (natural, in view of Mr. Hayward's hand in its
design) to the classically refined model evolved by the
Cambridge University Press for his National Book League
Catalogue, *English Poetry* (1947). Collations are given of
all copies listed as first editions; bindings are fully described; bibliographical references are ample; and scrupulous
attention has been paid to provenance. In addition to these
standard features, analytical and bibliographical annotation
has been generously provided for any book which seemed
to need it. Many did: there are important contributions to
the bibliographies of Boswell, Fielding, Gay, Hume, Prior,
Smollett (though not, unfortunately, for *Humphry Clinker*)

and above all Swift. Indeed "Rothschild" will be a required neighbour to "Pforzheimer" on any serious bibliographical reference shelf.

Lord Rothschild was obedient to the dictates of contemporary taste in the matter of original condition, and his library contains an astonishingly high proportion of copies in original boards or wrappers, or stitched or stabbed uncut, as issued. Nor was he insensitive to the charm of "association": here is Berkeley's *Siris* annotated by Blake; Cowper's *Poems* presented to Mrs. Unwin; Walpole's copy, with prolific notes, of Bubb Dodington's diary and (*O altitudo*) his annotated copy of Gray's *Odes*, the first book printed at Strawberry Hill; a presentation copy of *Rasselas* to Cornelia Knight, who wrote a sequel to it; Shenstone's copy, with his notes, of Prior's *Poems on Several Occasions*; and many others. There are more than a score of items either hitherto unrecorded or, if recorded, unique or one of two or three known; and the conservative care with which the adjective "unique" has been used is exemplified in a number of instances where copies hitherto described by the authorities as unique have been shown by the compilers to be not so. It must suffice to mention a mere handful of these *rarissima*; the *Proposals* for a two-volume edition of Boswell's works [*c.* 1767], Fielding's *Stultus versus Sapientem*, 1749, Swift's *The Fable of Midas*, 1712, all unique; Burke's *Essay towards an Abridgment of the English History* [1757], one of two known;[1] trial printing (*a*) of the first of the Drapier Letters, 1723–24, one of two copies, and trial printing (*b*) of the same, unique. These last will recall Lord Rothschild's learned paper of 1938 on the most crucial of the many *cruces* in the bibliography of Swift.

The catalogue contains 2,739 pieces, including the

[1] Publication of this article produced a letter (*TLS*, 27 May 1955) adding a third, in the library of the Constitutional Club, London.

products of the esteemed presses and the bindings (among which the Roger Paynes are predominant), but excluding the contents of the special collections. The major collections are those of Boswell, Fanny Burney, Defoe, Fielding, Gay, Gibbon, Goldsmith, Gray, Hume, Pope, Prior, Ramsay (though many not first editions), Richardson, Smart, Smollett and Steele, who are present virtually complete in first edition, with many variant issues and significant later editions. The Swift collection, richer than all the others in manuscripts and *rariora*, is in a class by itself. It must be doubted (with a bow to Sir Harold Williams) whether it is—or indeed now could be—surpassed, or even equalled, in private hands.

The representation of secondary and minor authors is variable. Colman and M. G. Lewis, for instance, are thin, and Beckford very thin (no Lausanne *Vathek*, no *Azemia* or *Modern Novel-Writing*). There are some noticeable absentees: Berkeley's *Treatise on the Principles of Human Knowledge*, *Grammont's Memoirs*, Mackenzie's *Man of Feeling*, Sheridan's *The Rivals*, Mrs. Inchbald's *A Simple Story*. There is no Crabbe, no Maria Edgeworth, no Regina Maria Roche (not to mention other "Gothick" novelists). And if room is found in a primarily literary collection for William Hunter, why not for John? There are also a few places where Lord Rothschild has been surprisingly content with an edition or an issue other than the first; Peter Beckford's *Thoughts on Hunting*, Burke's *Reflections on the Revolution in France*, two not unimportant and not impossibly rare tracts by Dr. Johnson, Raspe's *Baron Munchausen* (admittedly extremely rare), Shaftesbury's *Characteristics*.

It may seem captious to single out absentees from such a prodigiously fine collection. In fact it is a compliment, if a backhanded one, to the range and richness of the whole. Lord Rothschild makes no pretensions to completeness (why should he? how could he?) within his chosen range. The possessor of two copies of the Bristol *Lyrical Ballads* may view with equanimity the accusation that he has dispensed with a first edition of Garth's *Dispensary*. It is perhaps unreasonable, when we are given so much, to ask for more. Yet one does. To complete the canon of most of the authors only partially represented here would have demanded only a little more patience, only a little more determination, an expenditure equal to the difference between good and resplendent copies of half a dozen "high spots." And it would have made this catalogue something much closer to a descriptive bibliography of eighteenth-century English literature than it is, or, to be just, pretends to be.

No one has the right to criticize Lord Rothschild for the setting of his sights, nor even for deciding (if he did so), a dozen years after he had set his sights, that enough was enough. Yet his library gives more than sufficient evidence of planning, has so nearly approximated to the achievement of the apparent plan, that it must be judged by the most exacting standards of scholarship as well as connoisseurship.

To assemble a splendid collection, rich in rarities and masterpieces, and remarkable for its very high average of condition, is an enviable thing. To publish a scholarly and ample catalogue of it is an admirable thing. Many bibliophiles have done the former: a few the latter: and Lord Rothschild has an honoured place among the best of them. The very quality of his achievement, however, and still more its deliberate restriction of period and scope, inevitably (and perhaps to him unwillingly) provoke the question whether the Rothschild library has exerted, or will exert, any significant influence on the taste, as distinct from the technique, of other book-collectors. His design called for concentration rather than initiative, for devotion rather than imagination. He has ridden—and won—an extremely stylish race over a well-known course, rather than explored open country. It is doubtful whether, even in twice the dozen years of his activity, anyone could do what he set out to do, either in assembly or exposition, better than he has done it. And if he has had no ambition to open anyone else's eyes to unexplored avenues of bibliophily, who shall say that *incipit* is necessarily a more deserving word than *explicit*?

PART TWO

Two Typographers

DANIEL BERKELEY UPDIKE[1]

"Was Updike right," asks Mr. Ruari McLean in a recent number of *Signature*, "in not allowing his customers to give him instructions and never issuing a type book at all?" The question reflects, perhaps, a view of Updike not uncommonly held in this country, particularly among the younger generation: rather an autocrat; chilly, doctrinaire and patrician in temperament; meticulous, severe and a trifle unimaginative in workmanship. It is therefore well to be reminded that so great a stylist as Mr. Bruce Rogers referred as early as 1912 to his "unerring sense of style"; that his sharp eye put Janson and Bell types to use thirty years before the latter was even identified; and that when Mr. Rudolph Ruzicka once asked for his suggestions on the handling of some engravings for a Merrymount book Updike replied that "it was the printer's job to serve the material handed him, not the other way about."

Moreover, when Updike first set up for himself, in 1893, he set up as what we should now call a typographer. He was forced to invest in types, then to install compositors and so by reluctant stages to become a regular printer, not from any native taste or aptitude for a craft at which he was never mechanically expert ("to me all machinery is like a hideous form of algebra"), but because the contemporary attitude of those on whom he would otherwise have had

[1] This article was first published in *The Times Literary Supplement*, 20 March 1948.

to depend was well illustrated (the anecdote is recalled here [1] by Mr. Cleland) by the foreman who, studying his business card, said: "Updike... Updike. Oh, you're the fellow who does the queer printing, aren't you?" Yet the typographer's reply was equally revealing. "Perhaps," he said; "but will you permit me to remind you that your printing looks as queer to me as mine possibly can to you."

There was, certainly, something in Updike's temperament which explains his reputation for being autocratic. No book-designer or printer could want for a better motto than his: *Optimum vix satis*. No man, whatever his trade, could improve on the "simple idea" that in the very beginning "got hold of" Updike—"to make work better for its purpose than was commonly thought worth while." And whether it be true, as Mr. David T. Pottinger claims, that Updike was "the peer of the great typographers," he was eminently successful in the achievement of his stated ambition, which was "to do the ordinary work of its day well and suitably for the purpose for which it is intended." That the result often achieved a quality (again in his own words) "so agreeable to its purpose as to appear inevitable" comported with his conviction that "the beauty of any piece of printing is almost always the by-product of its adaptation to its purpose": but that it sometimes had beauty as well, was due to his own discriminatingly traditionalist sense of style. And the virtues of that style—clarity, regularity and dignity—had, as Mr. Beilenson notes, their roots in the printer's nature. To understand something of Updike's character and the circumstances of his early life is more

[1] *Updike: American Printer, and his Merrymount Press* (Notes on the Press, and its Work by Daniel Berkeley Updike: with a Gathering of Essays by Stanley Morison, Gregg Anderson, T. M. Cleland, M. A. de Wolfe Howe, George Parker Winship, Rudolph Ruzicka, David T. Pottinger, Carl P. Rollins: edited by Peter Beilenson). New York: The American Institute of Graphic Arts.

George Parker Winship: *Daniel Berkeley Updike and the Merrymount Press of Boston, Massachusetts.* Rochester, New York: Leo Hart.

than ordinarily necessary to the appreciation of his work;
the glimpses which he occasionally allows us in his own
"Notes on the Press and its Work" are valuably supple-
mented in several of the essays by other hands here printed
or reprinted with them.

The scion of an old Rhode Island family—a vigorous
line of religious colonists—he matured in Boston: a combination wherein Back Bay or Newport more than holds
its own with the world of the Forsytes or the Faubourg.
And the compensation exacted by his extreme shyness,
aggravated as it was by physical frailty, took the form first
of recourse to religion and secondly of the imposition (as
Mr. Beilenson puts it) of "his *consciously* superior taste and
training on those few parts of [life]—like printing—with
which he *chose* to deal." The words here italicized offer
a significant clue not only to Updike the man, but also to
his product. It was not that he in any way condescended.
But he took the measure, like the New Englander he was,
of a particular kind of job, and he carefully limited the
range within which it could be done well by his standards.
Those standards, as befitted a product of Providence and
Boston, were uncompromisingly severe and studiously un-
pretentious. That they were lived up to without the
smallest deviation of aim, whatever may have seemed to
him shortcomings of performance, was undoubtedly cause
for quiet satisfaction to the octogenarian founder of the
Merrymount Press. But it was characteristic that when in
1928 an exhibition of Updike's printing was put on in New
York, he absented himself from the opening "on the
principle that one would rather have it asked why one was
not, than why one was, there."

In the following year Mr. G. P. Winship wrote that
Updike had "done all the kinds of work that he said
he wanted to do, and comparatively little else." This
remained true. Updike as a book-designer was seldom

imaginative or inventive, and never revolutionary. His work sometimes seemed so austere, so astringent, that (like a very dry Tio Pepe) it was almost without flavour. But to the typography of a country which never lacks enterprise, colour and ebullience he has left an invaluable legacy: the firmly laid foundations of an academic style at once rational and urbane, and a body of work which consistently exemplifies his special quality—a sense of order, of self-discipline, of dignity. That there is being produced today at Princeton, at Harvard, at Chicago and elsewhere scholarly printing of a steady excellence is largely due to the assimilation of Updike's principles: while his standard of presswork was unrivalled in America and unsurpassed by Edinburgh or Cambridge.

Due in no small measure to the fact that a large proportion of Updike's most carefully pondered work was produced for private or institutional circulation, he is much better known in this country as a historian than as a practitioner. And indeed the comprehensive scope, the learning, the ripe judgment, the witty style which have made his *Printing Types* an indispensable book in several professions would have been enough to keep the name of Updike in honour if he had never designed a page in his life. Consequently, though books about printers are no substitute for books made by printers, Mr. Beilenson's tactfully assembled volume deserves a special welcome in Europe. A series of text pages from Merrymount books would probably have pleased their printer better than the title-pages reproduced here, interesting though some of these are. But his fine and prescient taste in type-faces is eloquently demonstrated in the dated specimens prepared by his partner, Mr. John Bianchi (about whom the reader would like to know more).

STANLEY MORISON [1]

MR. STANLEY MORISON, commonly but inadequately known as "the man who redesigned *The Times*," has consistently rejected the description of "typographer." First of all, therefore, I want to consider what we mean by the word, and then to justify its application to him. To the average man, a typographer, if he has heard of the animal at all, is someone who puts in the curlicues which distinguish "fine" printing from printing. To a good many printers he is an amateur theorist, full of damfool notions, who tries to teach veteran craftsmen their business without knowing a kern from a quad. To the *Shorter Oxford English Dictionary* he is—simply, but at the same time vaguely—"one who is skilled in typography; a printer," and typography is "the art or practice of printing." The dictionary rightly avoids specifying the printing of *what*: for typography is an art of arrangement as directly concerned with the lettering and pictorial matter on the package of cereal on our breakfast table, the placards to which we are exposed on our way to work, or the letter-headings in the morning's post at the office, as it is to the book or magazine we take up from the bedside table at night.

As for its practitioners, no one has in fact improved on the definition offered by Joseph Moxon, who produced in 1683 the first practical treatise on printing to be published in England.

> By a typographer [he wrote] I do not mean a printer, as he is vulgarly accounted: I mean such a one, who by his own judgment, from solid reasoning within himself, can either

[1] This piece was first given as a talk on the Third Programme of the B.B.C. in 1949, the year of Mr. Morison's sixtieth birthday. It was subsequently printed in the *Publishers' Weekly*, New York.

perform or direct others to perform, from the beginning to the end, all the handy-works and physical operations relating to typographie.

Mr. Morison's diffidence in assuming the title of typographer derives partly from a temperamental preference for the role of backroom boy or *éminence grise*, partly from the fact that he was never trained in "all the handy-works" to the craft; though there must be few printers today bul would acknowledge his technical mastery of the manuaf and mechanical operations involved in the immensely various and complicated business of modern printing. But if we choose to overrule him, and to insist on placing him among the most influential typographers of our time, we may rest our case on one phrase of Moxon's which is more peculiarly applicable to Mr. Morison and his work than to any of his contemporaries; or indeed to any of his predecessors since his acknowledged masters, the brothers Didot. For it was from "solid reasoning within himself" that Morison evolved, during his formative years from 1913 to 1923, those principles of typography which he has steadfastly practised, and caused to be practised by others, during the succeeding quarter of a century.

John Dreyfus, in an article in *Signature* on Morison's development as a typographer, perceptively observed that there is a Newtonian touch in Moxon's phrase. For Morison is not only a born rationalist: he also possesses, to a degree rare in this age of specialists, that fertile, wide-ranging, sceptical curiosity, as practical as philosophical, which characterized the age of Newton, Wren and Hooke. His attitude to conventions as such, whether in the editing of a book, the organization of a newspaper, the layout of an advertisement, or the disposition of "prelims," is ruthlessly clear-eyed: yet his respect for tradition and order is profound. It is well exemplified in some remarks of his about type design, a component of contemporary typography which owes more to Morison than to any single living man.

Type design [he wrote in 1930] moves at the pace of the most conservative reader. The good type-designer therefore realizes that, for a new fount to be successful, it has to be so good that only very few recognize its novelty. If readers do not notice the consummate reticence and rare discipline of a new type, it is probably a good letter. But if my friends think that the tail of my lower-case r or the lip of my lower-case e is rather jolly, you may know that the fount would have been better had neither been made. A type which is to have anything like a present, let alone a future, will neither be very "different" nor very "jolly."

To the amateurs of "fine printing," this austere doctrine might sound like the antithesis of all that their idol, William Morris, is thought to stand for. So, indeed, might Morison's astringent definition of typography itself, as "the efficient means to an essentially utilitarian and only accidentally aesthetic end." In reality no such antithesis exists between the principles of the two men, however widely some of their productions differ; and in an address delivered in 1944, at the Edinburgh College of Art, Morison was at pains to rescue William Morris, for whom he has the warmest respect, from the misconceptions of his more uncritical admirers. I will quote two sentences from that address. "If you want to publish a handsome edition of a book as well as a cheap one, do so; but let them be two books; and if you (or the public) cannot afford this, spend your ingenuity and your money in making the cheap book as sightly as you can." And again—"books whose only ornament is the necessary and essential beauty which arises out of the fitness of a piece of craftsmanship for the use for which it is made." Two more Morisonian sentiments it would be hard to find. Yet they were both in fact expressed by the printer of the Kelmscott Chaucer.

Among more recent typographers, theorists, and fosterers of sound principles in printing, Morison has acknowledged his debt to Gerard Meynell and the group of revolutionaries who founded the *Imprint* in 1913—that first concerted effort to carry the revival into the wider fields of commercial printing; to A. W. Pollard, of the British Museum, who directed his attention to the French printers of the sixteenth century—a potent source of later inspiration; and to those two great American writers on typography, Theodore L. de Vinne and Daniel Berkeley Updike. The affinity with Updike in particular was both close and peculiar: close because the two men had in common certain fixed principles of discipline and order in typography, and a notable inflexibility in enforcing them; peculiar because each combined in a rare degree the capacity for historical research and its luminous exposition with the capacity for putting the results of research into practice. Nothing of Morison's is so comprehensive as Updike's great book *Printing Types; their History, Forms and Use*, but he has been incomparably more prolific. The list of his published output runs to over 130 entries, including more than twenty books. Its contents range in date of subject from a penetrating suggestion on the origin of Latin uncial script in the third century A.D. to an estimate of the importance of photo-composition, a process still in the embryo stage in 1950. Its scope is probably wider than that of any other authority on letters and their arrangement, living or dead. And it includes half a dozen volumes, with perhaps twice as many papers or introductions, which are recognized by those equipped to judge as landmarks in the literature of the printed, written, or engraved word.[1]

[1] See *A Handlist of the Writings of Stanley Morison*, compiled by John Carter, with some notes by Mr. Morison and indexes by Graham Pollard. Cambridge, printed at the University Press for private distribution, 1950.

It is Morison's broad view of the relation between different kinds of letter-forms and their arrangement—whether incised on stone or metal or wood; written with the quill or reed or pen on vellum or paper; multiplied by types cast from matrices struck by engraved punches; or reproduced by one of the numerous photographic processes—it is this horizontal as well as vertical approach which gives his interpretation of typographical developments its commanding force, and makes so persuasive his exposition of the principles and practice appropriate to typography's various mediums and purposes. These qualities can now be studied between a single pair of covers, in the Sylvan Press reprint of two essays of Morison's which sum up, perhaps finally, his typographical philosophy. His British Academy Lecture, delivered in 1937, shows the analytical historian at his mature best. His Edinburgh address of 1944 enlarges upon, and adapts to a student audience, those "First Principles of Typography" which had appeared in the last number of the *Fleuron* fourteen years before, and which, as separately reprinted, were saluted by Dr. John Johnson of Oxford as "the pocket testament of the craft."

Morison's combination of historical, expository and practical talents has been recognized by a so far unique "double": the gold medals of the Bibliographical Society (though he disclaims the title of bibliographer) and of the American Institute of Graphic Arts (though he has said that "the primary aim of printing is not to be an art, but to be the most responsible of ourso cial, industrial, and intellectual mechanisms"). But it is time to leave his contribution to typographical history and theory for his contribution to the printing practice of our time. This has been of three kinds: direct, in an immense volume of printed matter actually designed or supervised; indirect, by example and by precept; and indirect again, in a rather different way, through the provision of a number of first-rate type designs for mechanical composition.

John Baskerville was a writing master, an engraver, and the manager of a japanning plant before he took to the printing press. John Bell, his nearest rival in influence on English typography before 1800, was as much interested in newspapers and politics as in book-publishing. Morison, who greatly admires both men and who rescued Bell almost single-handed from a most undeserved oblivion, has a good deal in common with each of them. No man has more eagerly embraced the enlarged capacities offered by mechanical inventions, yet remained their discriminating master. No man of strictly disciplined mind and temper was ever less academic or had a greater relish for the world of affairs. Morison's large, but almost entirely anonymous, output in the field of book-design includes a number of volumes in the grand manner, which, like Baskerville's, have gone forth "to astonish all the librarians of Europe"—and of America. But it also includes a far greater number of high-class general books—for publishers who patronized the Cloister Press in the early twenties, for the Cambridge University Press, to which he was appointed typographical adviser in 1923, and for many others. Most numerously, perhaps, of all; most surprisingly, no doubt, to those who think of a typographer as a deckle-edged dilettante in a hand-set tower; but in complete congruity with the un-compromising rationalist philosophy of his "First Principles" and other theoretical writings of the twenties; Morison was the creator of the most effective, most economical, most Procrustean, and longest-lived "house style" in the history of book-publishing. I refer to the publications of the firm of Victor Gollancz Ltd, of which Morison was a director from 1929 to 1938.

The standardized Gollancz book—crown octavos printed in Baskerville, demys in Scotch Roman—in its

plain black binding lettered in Gill Sans, exemplified the
Morisonian principles of book typography at their
utilitarian ultimate. But it also provided, in its jacket, a
link with one of the several other Morisons: the Morison
who had learned at the Pelican Press with Francis Meynell,
in Manchester with Charles Hobson, what could be done
in jobbing and display printing by a man who combined
a really explosive conception of novelty with an imaginative eye for the typographical detonation of the explosions.
Morison's historic address on this subject to the Master
Printers' Conference at Blackpool in 1928 nearly caused a
riot. For printers are conservative folk, and Morison had
pushed his rationale of display and advertising typography
to logical conclusions as extreme, in their entirely different
way, as his ascetic code for book-work. "The typography
of books," he said, "requires an obedience to convention
which is almost absolute," so that "any disposition of
printing material which, whatever the intention, has the
effect of coming between author and reader, is wrong."
The typography of propaganda, commercial or other, he
conceived to be an utterly different matter. "It is the
proper business of effective business printing," he told the
Master Printers, "to include provocation among its con-
stituent virtues . . . to be effective, you must surprise—
startle." Anyone who analyses the studied wildness, the
cunningly contrived breaking of every accepted rule which
was itself the rule in the early Gollancz jackets, will
recognize the hand of a master-startler.

At the same time Morison, as typographical adviser to
the Monotype Corporation, was turning his researches into
the earlier history of type design to practical purpose.
Under his guidance were cut and made available to the
printing trade such now familiar founts as Monotype
Garamond, Poliphilus, Blado, Bembo, Fournier, Baskerville, and Bell. He acted as impresario for Eric Gill's

Sanserif, a type as firmly established today in jobbing and display work as is the same designer's beautiful Perpetua in book-work; and this was produced under similar circumstances. Last, and best known of all to the general public, is Times New Roman, a series of types requiring as many as 5,973 separate punches. This was specially designed and cut under Morison's direction as part of the restyling of *The Times* newspaper, which may perhaps be accounted (with one potential exception) [1] his most remarkable single achievement. It called into play almost all those different qualities the combination of which, under one rather disreputable black felt hat, makes Stanley Morison the phenomenon he is. He was thoroughly versed in the long history of newspaper production in this country, and was shortly to publish what immediately became the standard work on the subject—*The English Newspaper*. He understood not only what was required of a newspaper type but also, from practical experience, how to get it. His habit of mind equipped him to strike a just balance between respect for the comfort of readers accustomed to a familiar layout, and those improvements which a clear and rational eye for functional efficiency, lucidity and dignity perceived to be necessary. Finally, his grasp of these technical essentials was allied to a force of character, a contempt for personal credit, a robust common sense and a permanently functioning sense of humour, such as might well be needed to effect a revolutionary change in a proud and ancient institution.

Morison is on record as believing that "black letter is in design more homogeneous, more lively and more economic a type than the grey round roman we use," and he once produced a splendid folio to prove it. But he added that he did not now expect people to read a book in black letter; and he has in fact been instrumental in removing it from

---

[1] I was thinking of the *History of "The Times,"* of which Morison, anonymously, was editor-in-chief and part author.

many of its most familiar remaining footholds in our daily reading, namely the titling of newspapers, on the ground that it represented there an outmoded convention—the kind of thing with which he has no patience. After the august *Times* had taken the plunge, Morison himself was invited to design new headings for the *Daily Express*, the *Daily Herald*, the *Continental Daily Mail*, and the *Financial Times*; and his example has been followed by several other newspapers. He has more recently designed a whole series of forms for Cable and Wireless Ltd, and his satisfying hand may be seen also in the layout of the regular Post Office Telegraph forms.

In fact, I suppose there is probably no form of words arranged for human reading, from a bus ticket to a breviary, on which Morison could not—indeed, immediately would—offer a reasoned suggestion for improvement. He is not sparing of condemnation for shoddy, pretentious or ill-considered work. He recently opined, for instance, of the reproduction of some illustrations in a book produced by my own firm, that they would have been done better in Bulgaria. But he is equally generous with praise, especially for unobtrusive excellences. He is also generous with advice to those many friends and professional acquaintances—and nowadays a great many total strangers too—who have learned where best to seek it. And this not for books alone or newspapers or jobbing printing. If one wants to know who is the best man for a book label or a visiting card or a memorial tablet, Morison will always have a Stone or a Wolfenden or a Kindersley to recommend, and I have no doubt that if one were embarking on an advertising campaign which involved sky-writing, he would know of a pilot who had achieved—probably under his guidance—a tolerable command of the proper style.

For conclusion I cannot improve on the final paragraph of the article by John Dreyfus to which I have referred earlier—the considered tribute of a young typographer to a master.

Morison, John Dreyfus wrote,

has reminded printers of their duties to authors and to themselves, and has provided them with a variety of good types, and has shown how they should be used. It is a service for which any member of the reading public who "takes print for granted" should be grateful. . . . Those who work with him observe that he does not claim to "feel," but is content to think, that a certain form is the most appropriate to impose upon a given piece of "copy," and he will produce his reasons for so thinking. It is a habit which leads him to demand reasons from those who propose alternatives. He is, in fact, not a little stubborn in the use and defence of the methods he has found by experience to suit the work. He appears, also, to believe that the active and conscious application of the reasoning faculty to the problems of the printed page is an element in that intellectual hygiene but for which the mind, or at least his mind, might hesitate to put forth the effort to consider problems of a far higher order. Hence Morison may be described as, to use once again the words of Moxon, "such a one, who by his own judgment, from solid reasoning within himself," has elected to regard "Typographie" less as an opportunity for self-expression, as the word is commonly understood, than as a means of self-discipline.

PART THREE

Five Essays in Bibliophily

COLLECTING DETECTIVE FICTION [1]

Note. Detectives and other fictional characters are distinguished from authors, etc., by being put into italics.

THE detective story shows every sign of having come to stay. As a literary form it is not yet 100 years old, and there have not been wanting during its most recent heyday (which is still going on) certain crabbed persons to prophesy that such a boom must end in a slump, with the implied, or sometimes explicit, rider that the sooner this happens the better for the republic of letters. But even if the output of detective stories stopped tomorrow, the vogue has been long enough and prolific enough for the production of a body of literature which the Taines and Saintsburys of the future will not be able to ignore, even should they wish. In point of fact, there is no reason why they should wish. For quite apart from the distinguished authors scattered up and down its history, it is notorious that the detective story is the favourite reading of statesmen, of dons in our older universities, and in fact of all that is most intellectual in the reading public. The late Lord Rosebery possessed a first edition of *The Memoirs of Sherlock Holmes*, and Philip Guedalla is credited [2] with stating that "the detective story is the normal recreation of noble minds." The Provost of Eton[3] is an acknowledged

---

[1] This essay was first published, with much bibliographica ldetail here omitted, in *New Paths in Book-Collecting* (Constable, 1934) and later reissued separately in the same publisher's Aspects of Book-Collecting series.

[2] Falsely, he subsequently told me.

[3] The late Montague Rhodes James.

authority on this, as on so many other subjects; Mr. Desmond MacCarthy is a prominent Holmesian scholar; and the Secretary to the Syndics of the Cambridge University Press [1] is responsible for the standard life of *Doctor Watson*.[2]

If we err, therefore, in our liking for detective stories, we err with Plato.

But if we are pleased to take them reasonably seriously, our first consideration must be to distinguish the detective story proper from the various types of literature which are its first cousins on one side or the other. This may not be essential to the reader, but the collector, even one with ample shelf-room, will probably find himself, amongst such a wealth of kindred material, compelled to reserve his energies and space for the genuine article only. On the one hand, then, he will avoid criminology; any records of actual facts. This principle need not necessarily exclude fiction based on fact, like Poe's *The Mystery of Marie Roget* or Wilkie Collins's *The Moonstone*. The former, as is well known, was constructed from the newspaper accounts of an investigation proceeding at the time in New York, and the paper which published Poe's story did not dare, for very good reason, to take it as far as his conclusion. It is said that, years later, the confession of the persons he indicated confirmed the accuracy of his solution. As for *The Moonstone*, several incidents and the detective himself —the immortal *Sergeant Cuff*—were lifted from the sensational Constance Kent case, which had taken place a few years earlier. Nor need fiction masquerading as fact be barred. Some of the many volumes which appeared in London from the fifties onwards, purporting to be reminiscences, may actually have been genuine; but the

---

[1] Mr. S. C. Roberts, now Master of Pembroke College, Cambridge.
[2] I might have added that Vizetelly, on his English translations, advertised Gaboriau as being "the favourite reading of Count Bismarck."

authors of most of them were literary hacks, and it is probably safe to label the whole class of "Revelations" and "Experiences" and "Diaries" of "Real Detectives" and "Ex-detectives" as fiction, at any rate down to 1890.

At the other end of the scale the line is often much more difficult to draw. Many uncritical people, if suddenly asked to name a modern writer of detective stories, would offer Edgar Wallace; but in fact Wallace wrote very few detective stories proper. If we decide, as surely we must, that a detective story within the meaning of the act must be mainly occupied with detection and must contain a proper detective (whether amateur or professional), it is clear that mystery stories, crime stories, spy stories, shockers, even Secret Service stories, will have to be excluded unless any particular example can show some authentic detective strain. We may choose to admit to our collection *The Four Just Men* or *Raffles* or *The Thirty-Nine Steps*, but it must be realized (unless we are prepared for their logical results —to the tune of several thousand volumes) that they are there as a matter of grace and not of right.

Considering that all the historical and literary criticism of the detective story is the product of so short a period as the last eight years [1] only, the subject is singularly fortunate in the commentators it has attracted. The specialists in the exegesis and chronology of the *Sherlock Holmes* cycle are perhaps rather advanced for the layman, who often finds the higher criticism wearisome, to whatever it is applied; but if Mr. H. W. Bell's thoroughness is terrifying, others besides Conan Doyle enthusiasts enjoy Father Ronald Knox's erudite virtuosity.

Of workers in the field as a whole four names stand out. The late E. M. Wrong, Fellow of Magdalen College,

---

[1] This remember, was written in 1934.

Oxford, and a distinguished historian, introduced his selection of *Crime and Detection* in the World's Classics series with an essay, analytical, philosophical and historical, which remains the best thing yet written on the subject. Willard Huntington Wright, who is probably better known by his pen name of S. S. van Dine, introduced a bulkier anthology in the following year with an excellently balanced survey, which has for our present purpose this advantage over Wrong's that it is packed with detail. In 1928 Miss Dorothy Sayers, in a similar role, proved herself as distinguished a critic and historian as she is a creative artist. And in 1931 Mr. H. Douglas Thomson produced, in a work whose title (*Masters of Mystery*) belies its merits, the first full-length study of the detective story.

Although there have been other, mostly critical, contributions from such writers as G. K. Chesterton, Father Knox, and Vernon Rendall, these four authors are our main authorities for the general history and development of the detective story.

The main outline is familiar enough. There have been attempts, it is true, to establish Herodotus, Sophocles and the authors of certain books of the Apocrypha as early exponents of the detective story. But these are hardly justified; and though we today may account it strange that there were no true examples of the form before 1840, it is usually and rightly held that it originated with Edgar Allan Poe. Poe's three great stories touched a level of excellence very remarkable in view of their incunabular position and one to which no other writer attained for twenty-five years, even if (as some doubt) they have ever been equalled. Poe may have tired of his brilliant creation, or (and the lack of immediate successors in his own country makes this more likely) perhaps public response was lukewarm. At any rate it was not until Charles Dickens's interest in the recently created police detective force in London [1] had been communicated by him to Wilkie Collins, that we come to the next landmark. In 1868, however, appeared *The Moonstone*, which Mr. T. S. Eliot [2] has called "the first, the longest and the best of modern detective stories." Mr. Eliot is inaccurate in his first adjective, a little rash perhaps in his second, but unlikely to meet with much disagreement over his third. If Poe created the short detective story, Wilkie Collins is the undisputed father of the full-length variety, and it remained in the ascendant for higher class work until the arrival of *Sherlock Holmes*.

Meanwhile a star had arisen across the English Channel, and the novels of Emile Gaboriau took France by storm. *L'Affaire Lerouge* was published in *Le Pays* in 1866 and Gaboriau produced a number of equally famous successors to it before his death in 1873. He was followed by Fortuné de Boisgobey, whose novels, always full of dramatic incident, sometimes degenerate into mere sensational police stories; but at his infrequent best he was not unworthy of his acknowledged master. The influence of these two was more productive abroad than at home. There are few French detective stories of any note between Boisgobey's death in 1891 and the appearance of another pair of contemporaneous masters, MM. Leroux and Leblanc, about fifteen years later. Translations of Gaboriau and Boisgobey did not appear in London until the 1880's, but once launched in Vizetelly's cheap red-wrappered editions they

---

[1] Sir Robert Peel's creation of the police force dates from 1829, but it was only in 1845 that the germ of the Criminal Investigation Department (1876) was born. In that year Sir James Graham detailed twelve police officers for exclusive plain clothes detective work. Dickens was the first writer to recognize their importance, and he devoted four articles in *Household Words* (July–September 1850) to a description of their work.

[2] Introduction to the World's Classics edition, first issued in 1928 (No. 316). Mr. Eliot emphasizes Dickens's influences on Wilkie Collins at this time, and there is little doubt that in the unfinished *Edwin Drood* (1870) we have lost what might well have been a masterpiece of full-length detection.

sold in very large numbers, and their illustration of French police methods has had considerable influence in the development of what we regard today as the Crofts school of writers. But as one finds, unexpectedly, in the case of other of Vizetelly's continental importations, England waited on the United States; translations of Gaboriau had appeared in Boston and New York years before his fellow-countryman introduced them to London. They stimulated a public interest which rapidly evoked response in the form of native products, and though their influence on the celebrated Pinkerton series was probably no greater than that exerted by the numerous volumes of fictional memoirs which had pervaded the English bookstalls since 1855, it is plainly apparent in the work of Anna Katherine Green, whose vogue, beginning in earnest with *The Leavenworth Case* in 1878, remained the dominant feature of the American scene for several decades. Lawrence L. Lynch (Mrs. Murdoch van Deventer) was a fairly prolific runner-up, but although subsequent American writers were by no means idle, they contributed little of importance to the development of the *genre* until comparatively recent years.

In 1887 two remarkable events occurred, which make this year perhaps the most memorable in the whole history of detective fiction. The first was the sensational success of *The Mystery of a Hansom Cab*, by Fergus W. Hume. Published in Melbourne, Australia, the first edition of 5,000 copies was sold out in a week and others followed in quick succession; the publisher, Frederick Trischler, migrated with the book to London; the first London edition of 25,000 copies, issued over the imprint of the Hansom Cab Publishing Company, was exhausted in three days; and when the author died, in 1932, over half a million copies in all had been sold. No other detective story before or since can have touched such sale records, and it is not surprising that by the historians, as well as by the public,

Hume is today regarded as a one-book man. In fact, he wrote over a hundred other books, of which about half were detective stories, and if he is now not much read, his position in any historical survey is a significant one.

The other event of the year is unquestionably the more important.

In 1887 [wrote Miss Sayers in 1928] *A Study in Scarlet* was flung like a bombshell into the field of detective fiction, to be followed within a few short and brilliant years by the marvellous series of Sherlock Holmes short stories. The effect was electric. Conan Doyle took up the Poe formula and galvanized it into life and popularity.

Sherlock Holmes quickly reached, and has never lost, a position in the detective world which no other and abler practitioners have ever approached. It may be that we read these stories now less for their purely detective interest (always considerable) than for their masterly character drawing; it is true that the more fanatical tend to regard *Watson* as almost more important than *Holmes*, just as there are always some who attribute Socrates' quality to Plato or Johnson's to Boswell; but it is as impossible to exaggerate *Holmes's* pre-eminent influence over the next generation of detectives as it is to recreate that golden age when the public stood in queues at the bookstall for the new issue of the *Strand Magazine*. Conan Doyle has been a favourite with collectors for some years now, and as he has his own bibliographer the details of his books need not detain us. The resounding success of *Holmes* was the signal for a great increase in activity among detective story writers, and the last decade of the nineteenth century was favoured with a good deal of excellent work. *The Wrong Box* by R. L. Stevenson and Lloyd Osborne and *The Black Box Murder* by Maarten Maartens, both published in 1889, showed serious authors tackling the medium, and in 1894 Arthur Morrison introduced in *Martin Hewitt* the most considerable of *Holmes's* immediate successors. The work of L. T. Meade and Clifford Halifax proved that the combination of a novelist and a doctor could be a fruitful one, and the two series of *Stories from the Diary of a Doctor* marked the advance of scientific detection towards its most famous exponent, *Doctor Thorndyke*. M. P. Shiel's *Prince Zaleski* has many of the immortal *Dupin's* characteristics, and his talents are not unworthy of his prototype; but Mr. Shiel's books in collaboration with Louis Tracy are not up to the standards of either author working alone. Tracy has a number of good books to his credit, but his principal detective, *Furneaux*, was eclipsed by the rising stars of the new century.

In 1904 Arnold Bennett showed, in *The Grand Babylon Hotel*, that he could write an adventure-detective story as well as anybody; but he wrote no more. In 1907, however, Dr. R. Austin Freeman published through the obscure firm of Collingwood a book which marks a new level in scientific detection. *The Red Thumb Mark* introduced *Doctor Thorndyke*, whom Wrong considered "the greatest detective now in business," and it was only the first of a long series. *John Thorndyke's Cases* (Chatto & Windus, 1909) followed, and in *The Singing Bone* (Hodder & Stoughton, 1912) Dr. Freeman achieved one of his greatest triumphs with a series of stories in which the reader is first shown the crime being committed and afterwards accompanies *Thorndyke* in his solution. To waive the advantages of suspense and surprise is a severe test for any detective author, but in the event these are among Freeman's best stories.

Baroness Orczy's *The Old Man in the Corner* (Greening, 1908) is an early and persuasive example of the intuitive school of detectives, which has become better known through the work of G. K. Chesterton's Roman Catholic priest, *Father Brown*; and, more lately, by H. C. Bailey's series of books describing the exploits of *Reginald Fortune*, whose conversational powers prevent some people from estimating his talent as dispassionately as they otherwise might. Ernest Bramah's *Max Carrados*, being blind, is to some extent inevitably intuitive, but his methods in general are as ruthlessly logical as the purist could wish.

With A. E. W. Mason's *Hanaud* in 1910 we return to a really great policeman, after a period in which the amateur or the private agent had been practically in possession of the field. *At the Villa Rose* was followed by *The House of the Arrow* and *The Prisoner in the Opal*, but their author had other fish to fry and we have not had as many of *Hanaud's* cases as could be wished.

In 1913 what may be called the *Sherlock Holmes* period comes to an end; and it ends with a book which can hold its own with any detective story ever written—E. C. Bentley's *Trent's Last Case* (Nelson, 1913).

The European War put an effective stop to the production of detective fiction, but its revival was signalized in 1920 by the appearance of *The Cask* by Freeman Wills Crofts; a book not only of remarkable quality but also one which has profoundly influenced the modern detective story as a whole. Mr. Crofts combined the elaboration of Gaboriau with an integrity of method which set an altogether new standard for the many police detectives who have followed *Inspector French*. The amount of patient work *French* gets through is often too much for the reader who wants entertainment rather than intellectual exercise, but it gives an effect of realism which is an indispensable quality; and in practice his scrupulous care for details, especially of time, produces remarkable results, so that one critic has observed that any character in a Crofts novel who has an absolutely impregnable alibi becomes *ipso facto* an object of immediate suspicion to the reader. *The Cask* did not reach a second edition until 1921, and the first, a small one, is extremely scarce. *The Ponson Case*, which seems to be even scarcer, appeared in 1921, and *The Pit Prop Syndicate* in the following year; and although *French* was then joined by a number of distinguished rivals, he has continued to add workmanlike cases to his record.

The years from 1920 onwards introduce one by one names which are now household words in detective fiction. 1920, Agatha Christie (*The Mysterious Affair at Styles*, New York, Lane); 1921, Eden Phillpotts (*The Grey Room*, New York, Macmillan); 1922, A. A. Milne (*The Red House Mystery*, Methuen); 1923, Dorothy Sayers (*Whose Body?*, New York, Boni & Liveright) and G. D. H. Cole (*The Brooklyn Murders*, Collins); 1924, Philip Macdonald (*The Rasp*, Collins) and Lynn Brock (*The Deductions oj Colonel Gore*, Collins); 1925, Anthony Berkeley (*The Layton Court Mystery*, Jenkins: published anonymously), Ronald Knox (*The Viaduct Murder*, Methuen); 1926, Henry Wade (*The Verdict of You All*, Constable); and so on, down to the present day. The later books by these authors are too well known to need listing here; and as for others, the output of the last ten years [1] has been so enormous, the general level of quality is so high, and the widely various enthusiasms of the *cognoscenti* are so intemperate, that a selection would be as rash as it would be impractical.

Of detective writers outside England since the Holmesian renaissance, there are only two Frenchmen of importance—Leblanc and Leroux. There are, however, a large number of Americans. It is true that until the last few years America has tended to lag behind England in the achievements and originality of method of her fictional detectives—what a poor figure Arthur Reeve's *Craig Kennedy* cuts, for instance, besides *Doctor Thorndyke*; but there have been plenty of good stories written by such authors as Melville Davisson Post, Mary Roberts Rine-

I.e. 1924–1933.

hart, John T. McIntyre and Isabel Ostrander (= also Robert Orr Chipperfield), and it is unfortunate that it is impossible to provide adequate bibliographical details here. But the difficulty of getting the books from across the Atlantic has been an insuperable obstruction, and the collector will have to wait for a prophet from their own country,[1] or do his investigating for himself. Mr. W. H. Wright treats them, as is fitting, more fully than our other authorities, and his information provides an excellent groundwork.

As for the moderns: Hammett, van Dine, Ellery Queen, Frances Noyes Hart and the rest; their names and works are as familiar as those of their English colleagues and it is equally unnecessary to insult the enthusiast by recapitulation.

The foregoing brief summary of the history of the detective story covers no ground unfamiliar to even the casual student of the subject, and it now remains to fill in a few of the gaps which the authorities have left unbridged. The literary critic and the historian rightly jump from one peak to another when they are describing their explorations to readers largely ignorant of the ground. But the collector is not only as much interested in the out-of-the-way books of all periods as in the familiar titles; he is also particularly curious about the early specimens of an afterwards popular and well-known literary form. There may be fifty detective stories published this year better than the best published in, say, 1860, but the interest of the latter lies, and very properly, in the fact that it represents a period in the history of the type about which the average collector is unlikely to know anything at all. "*Vixere fortes ante Agamemnona*," says Wrong, "but we have forgotten them, and tend to think of the pre-*Holmes* detectives as of the pre-Shakespearian

---

[1] E.g. Howard Haycraft, *Murder for Pleasure* (1942).

drama; to call them precursors only." This is true enough; and there are plenty of unregarded post-*Holmes* detectives, too, to attract the curious eye of the collector.

It was remarked above that police detection in England followed, at some distance, the disestablishment of the Bow Street Runners;[1] and although fictional reminiscences of the latter force are very rare, and not for our purpose very important, the large output of similar productions by, or purporting to be by, detectives and ex-detectives was a notable feature of those "dark ages," the 1850's and 1860's. These collections mostly appeared in the form of "yellow-backs" and they continued to find a public right down to the end of the century, but their complete omission from the history books is amply accounted for by their extraordinary rarity today, for which their perishable and ephemeral format was mainly responsible. Nevertheless, to skip gaily from Poe to *The Moonstone* is to ignore a large school of writers, whose influence and early date promote them to a position of importance usually, it is true, disproportionate to the quality of their work.

The most prolific author of this school was William Russell, who wrote under the name of "Waters." His best work was contained in the two series of *Recollections of a Detective Police Officer* (J. & C. Brown, 1856, and W. Kent, 1859), and the general character of the style is typified by the caption to the elegant frontispiece of the first volume— "The game is up, my good Mr. Gates, I arrest you for felony"—and by the quotation from Denman on the title page. This reads: "Police or Peace Officers are the lifeguards of the sleeping realm, without whom chambers would not be safe, nor the strong law of more potency than a bulrush." Russell's *Experiences of a French Detective*

---

[1] Griffiths (*Mysteries of Police and Crime*, 1898, Vol. 1, p. 129) says that "the old Bow Street Runner either retired from business or set up what we should now call private enquiry offices."

Officer "adapted from the MSS. of Theodore Duhamel" (Clarke [1861], Parlour Library, No. 234, pictorial boards or cloth) contains an Introduction explaining "The difference between English and French Detectives," which indeed a perusal of the text shows to have been badly needed; and among his other books are *Experiences of a Real Detective* by Inspector F. (Ward & Lock, 1862, Shilling Volume Library, printed wrappers); *The Autobiography of An English Detective* (two volumes, Maxwell, 1863, maroon cloth); *Undiscovered Crimes* (Ward & Lock, 1862, decorated wrappers); *Mrs. Waldegrave's Will and other Tales* (Ward, Lock & Tyler, Parlour Library Sixpenny Series, No. 14, pictorial wrappers [? 1870]); *A Skeleton in Every House* (Clarke [1860], Parlour Library, No. 222, pictorial boards or cloth). The tradition of Waters, Charles Martel, Andrew Forrester, Jr., and others of similar type was carried on by a host of later writers, few of whom stand out with any considerable run of titles. An exception is James McGovan, who produced a series of five extremely popular collections during the seventies and eighties. William Henderson, also a Scotsman, prefaced a similar volume in 1889 with a statement that "most of the so-called 'Experiences of Detective Officers' have had no foundation in fact." Inspector Moser, in *Stories from Scotland Yard* (Routledge, 1890), also insists that *his* tales "are all founded upon actual facts," and this tendency seems to have increased during the nineties.

In fact, towards the end of the century the "below stairs" school of detective fiction gradually split into two branches, as its chief vehicle, the yellow-back, became obsolete. On the one side it turned to fact; on the other it joined up with that huge stream of "bloods" which had run so strongly all through the Victorian period. Hogarth House, sponsors of *Jack Harkaway* and many other heroic figures, ran a department of their Gem Pocket Library which offered detective stories of "128 pages of new and original text, illustrated, in coloured wrappers" at twopence a volume. The People's Pocket Story Books were only threepence each, and the series contained many of the early exploits ot the celebrated *Nick Carter*, a detective who later gave his name to a weekly magazine and ran *Sexton Blake* [1] close for the blue ribbon of the popular-price field. Nor was the Aldine Publishing Company left behind: in May 1899 the titles in its series of Detective Tales (twopence each) had reached 256, and it numbered on its staff Detectives *Thrash* and *Pulcher*, *Harry Hunter* the Bootblack Detective, and *Daisy Bell* the Pavement Detective.

Turning to the more literary type of detective story, we find, as is natural, that fewer names have been overlooked by the historians, anyway before 1890, when the success of *Holmes* began seriously to affect output. *The Disappearance of Jeremiah Redworth* by Mrs. J. H. Riddell shows some interesting features for its early date (Routledge, [1878], pictorial wrappers), but it is much inferior to *Fort Minster, M.P., A Westminster Mystery* by Sir Edward J. Reed (Bristol, Arrowsmith, 1885, printed wrappers), in which the detective, *Strange*, gives a very capable performance. There are, moreover, in *Almack the Detective*, by E. H. Cragg ([The London Literary Society, 1886]), some remarkably early applications of scientific processes to detection, including deductions from blood corpuscles and microscopic photographs of the corpse's eyes, showing a blurred reflection of the murderer's face. H. F. Wood's *The Passenger from Scotland Yard* and *The Englishman of the Rue Cain* deserve to be noticed, as also does *The Queen Anne's Gate Mystery* by Richard Arkwright, if only for its modern-sounding title. "Dick Donovan" (Joyce Emerson

---

[1] Sexton Blake is the eponymous hero of what became a large syndicate of detective authors.

Muddock) is a much more considerable figure. Cast often in the form of the Waters-Martel "Reminiscences," his numerous books show a high level of competence, and they were extremely successful. *The Man-Hunter* (1888), *Caught at Last* (1889), *Tracked and Taken* (1890) were all published by Chatto & Windus, simultaneously in picture boards and in cloth. *The Man from Manchester* (1890) is a full-length novel, but in *Link by Link* (1893) Donovan returned to short stories. Milton Danvers produced a number of rather sensational stories during the nineties, published in pictorial boards or wrappers by Diprose & Bateman, and the work of such detectives as *John Pym* and *Michael Dred*, though derivative, is by no means contemptible. Max Pemberton and B. L. Farjeon both turned momentarily from other fields to the detective story, and Milne's Express Series included some examples good enough to make one wish it had had a longer life.

The work of Richard Marsh is more interesting, and in *The Datchet Diamonds*, *The Crime and the Criminal* and other books his touch is as effective in detection as it is in that well-known horror-story, *The Beetle*, on which his fame today is based. Headon Hill, too, ill deserves his oblivion: *Clues from a Detective's Camera* (Bristol, Arrowsmith, [1893], printed wrappers) and *Zambra the Detective* (Chatto & Windus, 1894) were followed by a number of other competently written stories.

There are innumerable lesser names, and it must suffice here to pick out half a dozen or so for mention. George R. Sims is chiefly remembered for *The Dagonet Ballads*, but he also wrote two detective books, *The Case of George Candlemas* (Chatto & Windus, 1899, pictorial wrappers) and *Dorcas Dene, Detective* (F. V. White, 1897, issued simultaneously in pictorial wrappers and in cloth). M. McDonnell Bodkin, Q.C., was responsible for *Paul Beck, the Rule of Thumb Detective*, and also for another lady detective, *Dora Myrl*.[1] G. W. Appleton, E. W. Hornung, the creator of Raffles, Burford Delannoy, A. C. Fox Davies, the authority on heraldry, Jacques Futrelle, Major Griffiths, Arthur W. Marchmont, all contributed work of merit; and one author, T. W. Hanshew, earns a niche apart as having written several detective novels in the style of Amanda McKittrick Ros, with results which have to be read to be believed. Finally, a tribute must be paid to a remarkable and inexplicably neglected book, *Thrilling Stories of the Railway* (Pearson, 1912, pictorial wrappers) by Victor L. Whitechurch, who later came into his own with *Shot on the Downs* and other detective stories.

These observations are based on the experience of only three or four years' serious attention to the collecting of detective fiction, and they are offered, therefore, with proper diffidence. Further attention, and the growth of public demand for the books, will no doubt bring to light many more bibliographical points, and will also probably modify any estimates of relative scarcity. I myself have had the greatest difficulty in running down copies of many *desiderata*, whether among those mentioned in this essay or among the many for which no space could be found here. And although the obscurer authors naturally give the most trouble, it is surprising how elusive several well-known titles by well-known authors have proved to be.

The evolution of a form of literature which is so much a part of our daily life as the detective story is a study as fascinating as it is deserving of serious attention, and from a collector's point of view it has a host of attractive features. The general outline, and the most important books, are fairly well known, but there are infinite opportunities for

[1] Lady detectives are uncommon and, on the whole, undistinguished. Other examples are found in Wilkie Collins's *No Name* (1862) and *The Law and the Lady* (1875); Baroness Orczy's *Lady Molly of Scotland Yard* (1910); and a curious American work, *Clarice Dyke the Female Detective.*

exploration among the obscurer authors and large tracts of practically virgin country. Detective stories have appeared in every kind of physical form from the full-dress three-volume novel down to the *Detective Supplement of The Union Jack*, and the prevalence of boarded or wrappered ephemera among the less literary and therefore socially and historically more interesting strata should whet the appetite of the keenest collector.

Finally, pioneer collecting of this kind has one very practical attraction to offer to its devotees. If it is stimulating to be ahead of the historian and the bibliographer, it is satisfactory to all of us, and a *sine qua non* to many of us, to be ahead of the market. In the few instances where the collector of detective fiction as such crosses the path of author collectors [1]—as for instance with Poe, Wilkie Collins and, to a less extent, Conan Doyle—he will, of course, find the prices already up: but over practically all the rest of the field he will find that though these books will cost him time, trouble and sometimes disappointment, they will not make much demand on his purse.

[1] He will also, as I myself can ruefully testify, run across Mr. Sadleir and his fellow-collectors of yellow-backs, and there the battle will be grim indeed, for these books are so rare that neither party, even alone, will find enough copies to go round: but it will be a competition of perseverance, not of purse.

OFF-SUBJECT BOOKS [1]

THERE are few things more fascinating to the reflective book-collector than the analysis of comparative rarity among books and the problems of its cause. Rarity is as it were of two kinds [2]—absolute rarity, and market, or temporary, rarity, and it is usually easier to determine the basis of the former than of the latter. A book may have been published in an edition of fifty copies, or suppressed on publication; or it may survive today in a total of five recorded copies only, from the mere obliviousness of previous centuries. It is sometimes possible to discover the reason for some unnatural scarcity—for instance, the bulk of the first edition of John Maynard Keynes's *The Economic Consequences of the Peace* (London, 1920) was lost at sea between the printers in Edinburgh and the publishers in London: and it has sometimes seemed proper to collectors or the booksellers to foster some perhaps apocryphal story of "a fire at the warehouse," as with the Third Folio of Shakespeare. But whether we can trace the cause or not, there are some books which have a definite, an absolute rarity, quite apart from any influence of public demand.

The much larger, and usually more interesting, class of rarities, however, comprises those books which have become difficult to find owing to some combination of circumstances in which the collector has himself played a part. The law of supply and demand can, in a surprisingly

[1] This essay was first published in the *Colophon*, New Series, Vol. I, No. 2, New York, 1935.

[2] Students of comparative scarcities who recognize this classification as over-simplified are referred to Chapter XI of my *Taste and Technique in Book-Collecting*, where they will find it much (perhaps too much) elaborated.

short time, produce a market scarcity of a quite common book, even if it be also quite well known. Other books are hard to find, and thus effectively, though not necessarily absolutely, scarce, from mere obscurity and the lack of any demand wide enough to coax them from the upper shelves. Then again there is a type of book which, though its author's work is sufficiently "esteemed" to put it in some considerable demand, happens to be on some subject remote from his usual field: and these books, often innocent of any apparent reason for absolute rarity, nearly always turn out to be a thorn in the flesh of the author-collector who aims at completeness.

There are two main reasons for this state of affairs. One is an obvious one: that such books, often issued by some other than his regular publisher, usually failed to appeal to the author's regular public, and so sold in small numbers. For instance, the innumerable readers of *King Solomon's Mines* and *She* were probably only mildly interested in Rider Haggard's *A Winter Pilgrimage, being an Account of Travels through Palestine, Italy and the Island of Cyprus, accomplished in the Year 1900* (London, 1901); and it is obvious that a devotion to *The Three Midshipmen* would be almost inevitably incompatible with any sort of enthusiasm for *Jovinian, or the Early Days of Papal Rome* (London, 1877), which nevertheless was also written by W. H. G. Kingston.

The other reason is a subtler one—the intersection of two currents of demand at one particular book. The earnest subject-collector who specializes in books on musical instruments has unaccountable difficulty in procuring *A Lost Art Revived: Cremona Violins and Varnish*, by a certain Charles Reade. The reason is that he has run up against the advancing phalanx of Reade collectors, of whose very existence he may well be quite unaware; and these on their side are equally hipped by the fact that some proportion

95

of the (probably already rather few) copies of the book have remained in the musical section of the average bookseller's stock. Similarly, the collector of Captain Mayne Reid expects, in the nature of things, to have difficulty in getting his first two novels, *The Rifle Rangers* and *The Scalp Hunters*, in any sort of decent condition, but his real troubles will be *Love's Martyr, A Tragedy* (Philadelphia, 1849) and *Croquet* (London, 1863)—the former because it was privately printed, the latter because it is even further from the author's normal field and is also subject to competition from collectors of books on croquet, who may not be numerous but will certainly be a grim and fanatical crew.

The position of these off-subject books as a class is perhaps worth a few moments of our attention; and we must begin by ruling out a number of authors—usually those who spring first to mind—who do not really contribute to it. "Miscellaneous writers," as the British Museum catalogue labels those whom it cannot classify, are clearly excluded, and *An History of the Earth and Animated Nature* (London, 1774), although heaven knows it was foreign enough to Goldsmith's genius, is yet not an off-subject book proper, from the fact that its author—poet, playwright, novelist and essayist in his own right—was also a hack-writer who had to turn his hand to any sort of work when times were hard.

Then many authors had two distinct lines; and even if they are today famous for their work in only one of them, their output in the other may be sufficiently large to put single representatives of it out of court. Milton, the author of *Paradise Lost* and *Lycidas*, was also a political pamphleteer. Lewis Carroll was also C. L. Dodgson. The author of *Nonsense Rhymes* was also *A Landscape Painter in Albania*. *Westward Ho!* is no more characteristic of Charles Kingsley's total output than *What Then Does Dr. Newman*

Mean? Conan Doyle is to me the creator of Sherlock Holmes, Brigadier Gerard and Sir Charles Tregellis; but to you he may be the writer on spiritualism who perpetrated some regrettable fiction in his youth. And by which of Mr. E. C. Bentley's two masterpieces will he be chiefly remembered by posterity—*Trent's Last Case* or *Biography for Beginners?*

Again, we must surely rule out two classes of book to which many authors (not poets or biographers) are prone —a volume of juvenile verse at the beginning, and a volume of reminiscences at the end of their career; though some collectors of bibliographies may make an exception of *Verses* by Mr. T. J. Wise (London, 1882).

Marginal cases are provided by authors universally known for one type of book who have indeed produced completely off-subject books, and of varying kinds, but in such number as to make a considerable part of their bibliography. Mr. Norman Douglas is a case in point, with his *Report on the Pumice Stone Industry in the Lipari Islands*, *The Herpetology of the Duchy of Baden* and a dozen other learned monographs quite unfamiliar to many who know *South Wind* by heart. And a still more difficult question is raised by an author whose off-subject book is his best known—for instance, Professor George Saintsbury's *Notes on a Cellar Book* is probably more widely read and loved than all his critical writings put together.

Of off-subject books proper, really freakish-seeming and isolated items in an author's output, a fair number are sufficiently well known to collectors in general and to collectors of the authors concerned in particular. *Text-Book of Biology* by H. G. Wells (London, [1893]); *The Scholar's Italian Book* by James Elroy Flecker (London, 1911); *How I Built Myself a House* by Thomas Hardy (in *Chambers' Journal*, 1865); *The Thermal Influence of Forests* by R. L. Stevenson (Edinburgh, 1873); *Movements in*

European History by D. H. Lawrence (London, 1921); *The Floral Telegraph* by Captain Marryat (London, 1836); *Lawyers and Legislators* or *Notes on the American Mining Companies* by Benjamin Disraeli (London, 1825); *The Allahakbarrie Book of Broadway Cricket for 1899*, by J. M. Barrie—these and a dozen more are familiar enough to those concerned. But the unfamiliar improbabilities are as curious as any of them. Who would have suspected J. S. Fletcher, doyen of detective fiction, of *A Short Life of Cardinal Newman* (London, 1890), or Marie Corelli of *An Open Letter to Cardinal Vaughan* (London, 1900)? Whether any prophetic gleams of the incorrigible Clovis are visible in *The Rise of the Russian Empire* by H. H. Munro (alias Saki) I do not know, but I defy the most diligent student of style to attribute *Dope Darling* by Leda Burke (London, [1919]) to its true author on internal evidence alone.[1] The fact that John Galt wrote *The Life and Administration of Cardinal Wolsey* (London, 1812), or Mrs. Gore, brightest of the "silver fork" novelists, *The Rose Fancier's Manual* (London, 1858), or Charlotte M. Yonge *A History of Christian Names* (2 vols., London, 1863) and *Friarswood Post-Office* (London, 1860), may be curious rather than exciting: but what lover of the sea can remain unmoved by the thought that *Representative Actors*, *A Collection of Criticism, Anecdotes etc.* (London, n.d.), however dull it may be, was written by W. Clark Russell? Who will not wish to set beside his first edition of *East Lynne* the same author's temperance tract *Danesbury House* (London, 1861)? What admirer of the work of Dr. John Thorndyke but will expect to find at least one red thumb mark in *Travels and Life in Ashanti and Jamin* (London, 1898) by R. Austin Freeman? Or what lover of the plough can grudge the loss of one farmer (*English Farming and Why I Turned It Up*, by Ernest

[1] Mr. Richard Garnett has since done so, and wins the cigar.

Bramah, London, 1894), which has given us Kai Lung and Max Carrados?

Charles Kingsley wrote *Hints to Stammerers* (London, 1864); R. M. Ballantyne wrote *How Not to Do It, A Manual for the Awkward Squad* (London, 1859); Professor Gilbert Murray wrote *Gobi or Shamo, A Story of Three Songs* (London, 1889); David Garnett abridged and adapted *The Kitchen Garden* (London, 1919); Jack C. Squire (apparently Sir John Squire) wrote *Socialism and Art* (London, [1907]); A. E. W. Mason wrote *The Royal Exchange* (London, 1920)—and so on and so forth.

Advertising brochures would reveal a quantity of interesting material, if only one could more often penetrate their anonymity—Hall Caine wrote a piece for the Isle of Man Steamship Line, Richard Le Gallienne a pamphlet on pillows; and the earliest work of Mr. Arthur Rackham is to be found in certain Norddeutscher Lloyd leaflets of the early nineties. But a name on a title-page is sometimes misleading. *Mental Furniture or the Adaptation of Knowledge for Man* and *The Vale Royal of England* were both written by Thomas Hughes; but their authors were two different Thomas Hugheses, and neither of them wrote *Tom Brown's Schooldays*.

These notes must be sufficient to indicate the possibilities of a curious and unexplored byway of book-collecting; but even the few examples which one observer has accumulated in a year or two of desultory search show clearly enough what curious and improbable collocations of author and title await us in unexpected corners. I should perhaps have been diffident of suggesting that here is yet another amusing "new path in book-collecting." But since writing the bulk of this article, I have seen some recent remarks to this very purpose by Mr. Michael Sadleir (who has inevitably stolen some of my fire-crackers in the process), so that any recommendations from me are superfluous. Yet whether we collect the books or not, the subject has the most fascinating possibilities. Who knows that Surtees did not write a volume of hymns or Bacon a treatise on anagrams?

COLLECTING A. E. HOUSMAN[1]

I SUPPOSE a good many booksellers do a little collecting on their own account, whether as a private demonstration of how it should be done, or to remind themselves that in the book business a professional can still be an amateur.

But where Dr. Rosenbach had his Juveniles and Mr. Goodspeed his Ruskins, most of us are perforce content to take our busman's holiday in humbler style. My own particular quest, pursued for some ten years now,[2] is Housman; and as the death of that remarkable man last year has set a term to an unusual bibliography, it may not come amiss to recall some of its less known constituents.[3]

Housman is an interesting author to collect for several reasons. First, there were, so to speak, two of him—the poet and the scholar. Now, in the case of Lewis Carroll, alias C. L. Dodgson, we respect (and perhaps collect) his mathematics and his logic only because they came from the same pen as *Alice's Adventures in Wonderland*, and not for (to most of us) any intrinsic interest. Similarly, if we buy the *Journal of a Landscape Painter in Albania* by Edward Lear, we shall indeed find it a delightful book, but we should never have heeded it had not Mr. Lear been also that "Derry Down Derry" who wrote and illustrated the inimitable *Nonsense Rhymes*. But not so with Housman, for he excelled in both his chosen fields. That he is a "major" poet may be disputable ("minor" he certainly is not). But that he is a poet of unusual quality, with a completely individual voice, will be denied by few; and surely

[1] This essay was first published in the *Colophon*, New Series, Vol. III, No. 1, New York, 1938.
[2] By now nearly thirty.
[3] See *A. E. Housman, An Annotated Handlist*, by John Carter and John Sparrow, Soho Bibliographies No. II, 1952.

none has combined more felicitously a romantic (often rustic) content with a Landorian classicism of form. As for his scholarship, he was by common consent the greatest Latinist of his age, and it will not be surprising if in the judgment of posterity he is found to stand with Bentley, Porson and Scaliger among the greatest names in the whole history of classical learning. Like some other poets, but like few scholars, he was also master of a forcible, lucid, and often picturesque prose style—a fact less familiar, maybe, to devotees of *A Shropshire Lad* than to those who have braced themselves in the keen wind which blows through the prefaces to *Manilius* and *Juvenal*, and those deadly, those magisterial reviews.

The other reason why Housman is particularly stimulating to the thorough-paced collector is that at first sight there is so little of him. There are three volumes of poetry, of which *Last Poems* (1922) and *More Poems* (1936) are despicably easy in first edition. *A Shropshire Lad* (1896) is not a common book—the London edition was three hundred and fifty, and a hundred and fifty more went to America with a John Lane, 1897, title-page—but the fact that it has for some years been a fairly expensive book means that if you have the money you can secure a reasonably good copy without much trouble. I do not possess one, and because this is one book of English poetry which I do not think will ever slump, I probably never shall.[1]

Then there are not many major classical works. Of the five volumes of *Manilius* (1903–1930) only the first is really uncommon today. *Juvenal* (1905) and *Lucan* (1926) complete the list of authors edited in separate form—with what a formidable array of *apparatus critici* and what still more formidable prefaces—and although both are scarce in first edition, neither is rare. I myself am not scholar enough to appreciate properly Housman's greatness as an

[1] I broke down in the end.

editor of Latin or as a commentator and emender of Greek texts; though at certain points it cannot but strike even the tyro, and I well remember the Olympian quality of his lectures at Cambridge. He never underlined a point, he never drew unnecessarily on the wealth of his unrivalled erudition, he never raised his voice (as he sometimes does in his critical writings), but one felt it quite impossible that he could ever be wrong. Indeed, I fancy that the dislike with which many contemporary scholars regarded him, particularly in Germany, was due not so much to the blasting way he had of castigating their work as to their inability ever to catch him out in return.

But the shortcomings of other scholars, of his own and of earlier days, provide for his readers a fearful joy. If Bentley was more ferocious, no one is more pungent, more incisive, more scorching in invective than Housman. And those who pass over his classical work under the impression that one must know Latin or Greek to enjoy it are missing not only some of his most remarkable writing, but also that always enjoyable experience—seeing somebody else being sent to the bottom of the class. Not that Housman was always depreciatory of other editors: far from it. He is invariably discriminating, and his praise is as justly apportioned, as generously bestowed and as admirably phrased as his censure. But it is also true that there is much less of it.

Those who esteem Housman the scholar and critic have long realized that the bulk of his work in this field was to be found in such learned periodicals as the *Classical Quarterly*, the *Classical Review* and the *Journal of Philology*. His contributions began in 1882, and they were throughout his middle years both frequent and considerable. Since there is to be no collected volume of his *adversaria* and reviews, collectors will still have to comb the files of the periodicals concerned to find much of Housman's pithiest and most characteristic prose; and they are fortunate in that Mr. A. S. F. Gow attached an exhaustive list of these contributions to his admirable memoir [1]—much the best sketch of Housman so far published and perhaps likely to remain so.

There are, however, one or two pieces less well known to collectors which deserve a mention. The Inaugural Lecture delivered at Cambridge in 1911 has never been printed—there was a reference which Housman could not verify—and I understand that it never will be. The *Introductory Lecture* delivered at University College, London, in 1892 has now been published (Cambridge University Press, 1937) and no doubt appreciated as it deserves, but it had been privately printed twice before. In 1933 it appeared in an edition of a hundred copies (Nos. 1 and 2 on blue paper), of which twenty-five were for the author and none for sale. This, except for one correction made by Housman, was a verbatim reprint of that *rarissima avis*, the original edition of 1892 (8vo, printed by the Cambridge University Press, issued stitched and without wrappers), of which only a dozen or so copies seem to have survived. As Housman's first separate publication this *Lecture* would be a highly desirable item, even if it were not, as it is, a remarkable piece of writing—an analysis of the value of the classics in general, and pure scholarship in particular, in education.

The only similar piece which I know of (apart from the familiar Leslie Stephen Lecture on *The Name and Nature of Poetry*, Cambridge, 1933) is an address delivered before the Classical Association in 1921. "I am obliged to be here [Cambridge] at the beginning of August for a meeting of the Classical Association, damn it," wrote Housman to a friend, reluctantly declining the suggestion of a gastronomical holiday in France; but he produced a splendid and characteristic paper entitled *The Application of Thought to*

[1] Cambridge University Press, 1936.

Textual Criticism,[1] the last sentence of which I cannot resist quoting:

> Knowledge is good, method is good, but one thing beyond all others is necessary; and that is to have a head, not a pumpkin, on your shoulders, and brains, not pudding, in your head.

Housman's verse translations from the classics provide a bridge between his two fields. Three of these (from Aeschylus, Sophocles and Euripides) appeared in 1890 in a volume of *Odes from the Greek Dramatists*, edited by his friend A. W. Pollard. Of this book (published by David Stott of London) there was an edition on large paper and an ordinary edition which is divisible into two issues, witness certain learned contributors to *Bibliographical Notes and Queries*. The binding, of white parchment boards, is usually much soiled. The famous "Fragment of a Greek Tragedy" (printed in the *Cornhill Magazine* for April 1901, and elsewhere) is not in fact a translation, though I have seen it catalogued as such by a reputable bookseller—it is an original work, and not only the best thing in Housman's lighter vein which has been so far published, but one of the most skilful and amusing of parodies.

The Quarto (No. 3, London, J. S. Virtue, 1897), however, provides us with the first printing of Housman's most interesting translation—that of Horace's "Diffugere Nives" (afterwards included in *More Poems*). And it is interesting not merely as his only version from the Latin which has been preserved to us, but also for another reason, best given in the words of a letter to *The Times* from one of his pupils:

> One morning in May 1914, when the trees in Cambridge were covered with blossom, he reached in his lecture Ode 7 in Horace's Fourth book, "Diffugere nives, redeunt iam gramina

[1] Proceedings, Vol. XVIII (1922), pp. 67–84.

campis." This ode he dissected with the usual display of brilliance, wit, and sarcasm. Then for the first time in two years he looked up at us, and in quite a different voice said: "I should like to spend the last few minutes considering this ode simply as poetry." Our previous experience of Professor Housman would have made us sure that he would regard such a proceeding as beneath contempt. He read the ode aloud with deep emotion, first in Latin and then in an English translation of his own. "That," he said hurriedly, almost like a man betraying a secret, "I regard as the most beautiful poem in ancient literature," and walked quickly out of the room.

No one, I think, will wonder that *The Quarto* is a favourite among my Housmaniana.

But we must leave the Kennedy Professor of Latin and turn to his *alter ego*, Terence Hearsay. Born in Worcestershire, Housman made Shropshire (where he never spent much time) so much his own that pilgrims feel a sense of grievance when they find that Hughley church has not, and never has had, a steeple: but they must "remember," as Housman himself said, "that Tyrtaeus was not a Spartan." None of the poems in *A Shropshire Lad* had ever, I think, been previously printed. But a few of the *Last* and *More* poems had appeared in periodicals or mixed volumes of verse, and the collector may be expected to take an interest in these earlier printings. "Her strong enchantments failing" and "Oh hard is the bed they have made him" ("Illic Jacet") both appeared, with somewhat different texts, in *The Edwardian* for December 1915; and "O youth whose heart is right" (*More Poems*, No. IV) in the April 1916 issue of the same magazine—the school paper of King Edward's School, Bath, where Housman's brother-in-law was a master. "Astronomy" ("The Wain upon the northern steep") was first printed in a volume called *Wayfarer's Love, contributions from living poets edited by the Duchess of Sutherland* (Westminster, Constable, 1894).

"The Oracles" ("'Tis mute, the word they went to hear") was first printed in *The Venture* (edited by Laurence Housman and Somerset Maugham, London, Baillie, 1903), "Epitaph on an Army of Mercenaries" was first printed in *The Times* of October 31, 1917; and it appeared in several anthologies (*Valour and Vision*, 1920, for example) before the publication of *Last Poems* in 1922.

Of *More Poems*, previous printings of the "Diffugere Nives" translation and "O youth whose heart is right" have already been mentioned. Of the final poem, entitled "Alta Quies," a slightly different version had appeared thirty-five years earlier, in *Waifs and Strays* (Oxford, Blackwell, Vol. II, No. VI, March 1881), under the title "Parta Quies"; and it may be noted that an error in punctuation (line 9) in the first impression of *More Poems* was corrected in the second. The penultimate poem, "For My Funeral," was first printed in the order of service for Housman's funeral at Cambridge (May 4, 1936). Three hundred copies of this were printed for the actual service, with a misprint (*Ecclesiasticus* for *Ecclesiastes* on p. [1]); one hundred more were printed some days later, with this misprint corrected, and a different initial O on p. [3]. The poem also appeared in several London evening papers on May 4th.

Of even greater interest, perhaps, are poems in periodicals, etc., which have not been included in any of the three volumes. There is a fourteen-stanza poem entitled "New Year's Eve" in the November 1881 number of *Waifs and Strays* (Vol. III, No. VIII)—that very scarce "terminal magazine of Oxford poetry" usually catalogued under Oscar Wilde, who was another contributor. Then the *Union Magazine* of University College, London, printed at one time and another three light poems, one of which, "The Amphisbaena" (June 1906), is now published, in a different version, in Mr. Laurence Housman's *A.E.H.*

The March 1911 issue contains not only a poem called "The Crocodile, or Public Decency," but also an inserted caricature of Housman which makes an interesting addition to his slender iconography. Then in 1930 two impudent young men produced, as a Christmas card for a few friends, thirty-seven copies of a leaflet entitled *A Fragment preserved by oral tradition and said to have been composed by A. E. Housman in a dream.* This was a single four-line stanza, reading:

> The bells jostle in the tower
> The hollow night amid,
> And on my tongue the taste is sour
> Of all I ever did.

Believing as they did that this was merely a very clever parody of Housman, they never dared to send him a copy. He could have corrected their belief, for the stanza duly appears (with authoritative differences of text) among the fragments printed from the poet's manuscript notebooks in Mr. Laurence Housman's memoir.

There were a few letters to the papers (chronicled by Mr. Gow); but apart from classical subjects and the Lectures already referred to, Housman's prose output was small. He contributed a delightful preface to the *Nine Essays* of his old friend Arthur Platt (Cambridge University Press, 1927); but more intriguing—to me—is an anonymous production dating from 1935. On the occasion of the Jubilee of King George V, Cambridge University was to offer a Loyal Address, and the composition of this was entrusted to Housman. It was published in the *Cambridge University Reporter* of May 14th, and treasured by those aware of its authorship. For official purposes, however, a few copies had been printed in folio, red and black; two on vellum (for the King and Queen), twenty-four on japon for the University dignitaries. It so happened that the Chancellor of the University at the time was Mr. Stanley Baldwin, who was sent a copy *ex officio*. It also happened that Mr. Baldwin's private secretary was a friend of mine and knew of my weakness for Housmaniana. So when he wrote to acknowledge receipt of the Address, he calmly added a command (the Chancellor was also the Prime Minister of England) that a second copy should be sent. It was sent—and it lies before me at this moment.

As I have told one story of pure luck in acquisition, I may be allowed to follow it with another (to disarm envy) of hard work. When I first heard of the 1892 *Introductory Lecture*, in 1929, I tried all the usual means of securing a copy. I was handicapped by the need for discretion, for in those days its very existence was unknown in the book trade, and I did not want to give too much away. I had no luck. I then wrote to the printers to ransack their basements. I wrote to University College, in case a copy or two remained on the shelves. I wrote to the author, who replied that he knew of no copies except his own and that in the British Museum. By this time I was on my mettle, so I decided to start from 1892 and work down. I learned that complimentary copies (the annual Lectures were not published) were usually sent out to the members of those faculties before whom they had been delivered—in this case, of Laws, Arts and Sciences. I secured the names of all such for 1892. I searched the learned reference books to locate the survivors—there were eleven that I could trace. I wrote to them all, to ask if they remembered the Lecture and if by any chance they had a spare copy. I got eleven replies—scholars are a courteous race. The first ten either didn't remember, or remembered but no longer had the pamphlet. The eleventh letter arrived on April 4, 1930.

I duly received a copy of the Lecture [wrote that eminent scholar, Professor A. F. Murison], but I will not sell it—not even to Rosenbach. However, I too am a bibliophile and I can appreciate your despair. I'll tell you what—I enclose it; and I make you a present of it.

If the reader feels that this was only good luck too, I am prepared to agree. But I had worked hard enough, I think, to have earned it.

Only one other department remains to be noticed—autograph and association material. Letters in Housman's beautiful autograph must survive in abundance; for apart from his ordinary correspondence he was unusually courteous in answering the importunity of strangers, he was famous for a quarter of a century, and he never seems to have employed either a typewriter or a secretary. His letters to his friends are delightful—racy, pungent and often gay—and even his more formal epistolary style shows constant flashes of the rapier.

Books from his library, the remnants of which were dispersed in 1936, very seldom bear his signature, and I was therefore particularly delighted to find it in his copies of *The Dolly Dialogues* (first edition, 1894), Rolfe's *Hadrian VII* and Bentley's *Biography for Beginners*—three favourites of my own. But to offset his reticence, he had the habit of making pencilled comments in the margins of his ordinary, as well as his professional, reading: as if that minutely critical faculty was never asleep. He seldom seems to have passed an inaccuracy or absurdity without some acid annotation, and anything which roused his dislike was liable to be mercilessly pilloried. On the title-page of Beck's *Index Euripideus*, for instance, against the long subtitle testifying to the completeness and accuracy of the work, Housman wrote simply "Liar and slave." And under the frontispiece to his copy of Francis Thompson's *Poems*, which mystically represents the Hound of Heaven, he wrote very neatly the caption "Three persons and one dog." But when I turned with lively expectation to *The Testament of Beauty*, sent to him with a fine inscription in Bridges's beautiful hand, I was disappointed. None of the leaves had even been opened.[1]

In the matter of signatures in his own books, Housman's practice was again characteristic. He almost never refused to sign a copy when requested by some admirer, for although he despised book-collectors he had beautiful and unexpectedly gentle manners. And as he despised printers too, he usually corrected and initialled any misprints into the bargain. But he was exceedingly sparing of real presentation copies of anything he wrote, as was perhaps to be expected in a nature so proud and so reserved: and in consequence, whereas merely signed Housman books are legion, genuine presentation copies are of the utmost rarity.

---

[1] Needless to say, there was a good reason for this. I subsequently acquired Bridges's covering letter of presentation and also Housman's draft of his reply, which reads, in part: "As you will have surmised, it comes too late to save my pocket; but I shall now be able to keep it uncut [even Housman was capable of imprecision: he meant unopened], and enlarge the fortune of my heirs." Since I bought the book for two guineas, the enlargement was not great.

BENTLEY THREE-DECKERS[1]

The name of Richard Bentley and Son, Publishers in Ordinary to Her Majesty Queen Victoria, is familiar to anyone who has interested himself in nineteenth-century fiction. From the early thirties, when the original Bentley was busy establishing himself as one of the most enterprising publishers of the day; through his partnership, and differences, with Henry Colburn; through the great price-cutting war with Routledge and others in the early fifties—the firm pursued its successful career to a point where, by the eighties, any novel published over the famous imprint commanded a pre-publication library sale which automatically put both author and publisher comfortably in the black.

The list contained its normal proportion of general literature, and from *The Ingoldsby Legends* in 1840 to Lord Roberts's *Forty One Years in India*, published in 1898, the last year of the firm's existence, had its full quota of best-sellers. But to most of us "Bentley" implies novels, novels in three-decker form, and usually, from the late seventies onwards, novels in some unusual style of binding: and those who saw the great Bentley collection of three-deckers in the auction room last week saw something which could probably not be paralleled anywhere—except perhaps in the novel room of the old Cambridge University Library.

The firm of Bentley, taken over by Macmillan in 1898, seems so essentially Victorian that it was hard for those who met him to realize that Mr. Richard Bentley, of Upton, Bucks, who was alive and remarkably vigorous

[1] This article was first published in the *Spectator*, 7 May 1937.

until 1936, had been for many years in the family business,
retiring only with the disappearance of the imprint. But
for anyone who had the good fortune to know him, a rich
vein of genial reminiscence was there for skilful tapping—
anecdotes of Marie Corelli, trade gossip and customs of the
eighties, what Mr. Mudie said about George Moore, or
why the scarlet bows appear on some copies only of *Wormwood*. Mr. Bentley was a beautifully eccentric old gentleman, and much of the upper part of his house was fitted
up like the interior of a ship. These quarters he would
often show to visitors, and the original drawings for
Ingoldsby too. But penetration to the attic was a very
different affair, and it was several years before I myself
achieved it—it was too dark and cold, said Mr. Bentley, to
be attempted except at midsummer, and I could see for
myself that entry was made only by a ladder, a trapdoor,
and a stout rope of nautical style. One eventful day, however, my host, with an agility which more than abolished
the fifty years between us, led me up into an immensely
long attic, lined with glass shelves—and there was his
collection, his personal file, of the firm's fiction output, all
uncut, unopened and practically as new. It was a stagger-
ing sight for any eyes: to an amateur of the study of
publisher's cloth binding it was like a first glimpse of
Venice or the Parthenon, and the further one looked the
more fabulous seemed the array of gold and colour. Time
and damp, under the bright daylight of Messrs Hodgson's
sale room, were seen recently to have robbed some of the
earlier books of their brilliance; and the general condition
was not perhaps so incredible as that of the Bellew Library,
dispersed some years ago: but no one who saw the Bentley
file will ever forget it.

The earlier decades of the firm's activity were not by any
means fully represented, though to console us for the
absence of *Oliver Twist* (1838) there was indeed a copy of

The Last Days of Pompeii (1834) in one of the rarest of the six bindings in which the first edition occurs. The forties showed little of interest, but the fifties were dominated by Charles Reade, as were the sixties and seventies by Mrs. Henry Wood and Sheridan Le Fanu. Rhoda Broughton, Florence Marryat and Rosa N. Carey were present in full force; the Jessie Fothergills were headed by that rarity, *The First Violin* (1877–1878), in two issues, one of them previously unknown, and the Helen Mathers contingent by *Comin' Thro' the Rye* (1875). Marie Corelli was prominent in the eighties, and the turn of the decade produced the four earliest (and very scarce) novels of H. Seton Merriman, while two isolated titles deserve special mention—the first English edition of "Marcus Clarke's" *For the Term of His Natural Life* (1875), and the first production of a famous partnership, *An Irish Cousin* (1889), by E. Œ. Somerville and Martin Ross.

In general it must be confessed that Bentley's record as fiction publishers is more remarkable for its commercial success than for the uncovering of conspicuous talent, as may be gathered from the fact that all the "high-lights" have been mentioned above. In several cases, it is true, they nursed an author through his unprofitable period, only to have some other publisher make money out of him later. They were patient with Seton Merriman's early (and deserved) failures, but lost him to Smith Elder before *With Edged Tools*, his first really good book, and *The Sowers*, his best and most successful. They published Reade's earlier books (*Christie Johnstone*, by the way, was an absentee from the collection), but Trübner got *The Cloister and the Hearth* in 1861. Le Fanu, however, does the firm great credit: Bentley took over *The House by the Churchyard* from Tinsley (the "third" edition was merely the original sheets with a new title-page), published seven other of his novels between 1864 and 1872, and probably made no profit on any of them, except perhaps *Uncle Silas*. Yet 90 per cent of the novels in the collection have today no literary importance whatever, and 80 per cent would be entirely unknown to any but a professional student of minor Victorian fiction. And though few publishers would care to contemplate so severe a test as this Pisgah-sight of sixty-odd years' output, it is a chastening reflection that a successful fiction house should have sponsored so much triviality. But what they lack in literary content, the Bentley novels, from 1880 onwards at any rate, more than make up in their fanciful appearance. Fashionable ladies, they may be silly, but certainly they are exquisitely turned out.

The death-knell of the three-decker was sounded by George Moore and his publisher, Vizetelly, in 1886, when *A Modern Lover*, banished from decent shelves by Mr. Mudie in its three-volume, thirty-one-and-sixpenny form, was issued in a single volume at six shillings—to be bought, not borrowed from a library. The cheap new novel, attempted time and again, at last proved a practical publishing proposition; and though the three-decker persisted for ten years longer, it was doomed. But, thanks chiefly to Bentley and his binders, Messrs Burn, it died game, like a breaching whale, most magnificent in its last flurry. Between the cost of printing three heavily leaded volumes and the lowest trade price (50 per cent off the retail figure of a guinea and a half) lay a very handsome margin. Mr. Bentley's lively fancy and Messrs Burn's technical ingenuity converted some of this surplus into a series of covers which made a Bentley novel recognizable anywhere. Peacock patterns, fancy stripes, lincrusta fabric; cloth fashioned to look like wood, like stone, like grass; visiting cards let into the sides, silk bows on the back, edges gauffred, zebraed, sprinkled with butterflies—no bizarre extravagance was too fantastic for Bentley.

I always like to think that it was the demise of the three-decker which decided Mr. Bentley to retire from publishing. If from the commercial point of view it was no longer a practical proposition, so also as a lay figure for decorative experiment it must have been almost exhausted: Bentley had given it a superb last fling. Mr. Mudie might probably have compared the performance to Nero fiddling while Rome was burning. Mr. Bentley's own simile was Mata Hari painting her mouth before the firing squad.

FASHIONS IN BOOK-COLLECTING[1]

FASHION, said Miss Elizabeth Hawes, is spinach. And in her fascinating chronicle of life in what is demurely called the rag-trade she constantly and firmly emphasized the distinction between fashion and style. I have not always found this distinction admitted by other experts in *la mode*, but it seems to one empirical observer at least to be a sound one; and, with similar allowance for overlapping, it has its analogy with the distinction between fashion and taste in the world of connoisseurship.

The seventeenth-century picture-lover's addiction to the Dutch and Flemish schools of painting was a widespread and deeply-based movement of taste. The vogue for Lely or for Kneller was a fashion, just as were more recently the vogues for Boldini or Sargent or Laurencin. Walter Pater illuminated a fresh aspect of the Renaissance, and Ruskin discovered Botticelli. But Mr. Berenson, for example, has not been content with critical appreciation and scholarship: he has also bestowed an accolade here, made a reputation there, invented a painter or two when necessary, setting fashions most successfully for those rich enough to follow them. The first Post-Impressionist exhibition in London, organized by Roger Fry in 1911, and the equally historic Armory Show in New York in 1913, were windows opened on to a new world, turning-points in the development of taste. But the Paris critics and dealers who then, as they still do, cried up (and priced up) one painter one year and

[1] This essay is an expansion, first published in the *Virginia Quarterly Review*, Vol. 26, No. 3, Charlottesville, Va., 1950, of an address previously delivered under the authority of the Antiquarian Booksellers' Association, and subsequently reprinted, in its present form, in *Talks on Book-Collecting*, edited by P. H. Muir, Cassell & Co., 1952.

another the next were as definitely occupied with fashion as Poiret or Dior or Balenciaga.

Architectural taste, whether expressed in construction or appreciation, shows similar fashionable excrescences at almost any period. Horace Walpole's Strawberry Hill was an influential piece of fashion-setting; so was Paxton's greenhouse at Chatsworth, quite apart from its technical significance. William Morris made handicraft fashionable, the bad as well as the good results of which we have with us still. The beautiful semicircular glass treatment of the stair-well in Gropius's Cologne Werkbund exhibition building of 1914 probably has by now one child or grandchild for every hundred square miles of Europe and America. And if Mr. John Betjeman has his way, it will soon be much safer for a young girl with intellectual aspirations to admire Keble College Chapel or St. Pancras Station than Chartres or St. Paul's.

When I was young the aesthetes and highbrows of my acquaintance were dedicated to Proust, to the collecting of Victorian lustre china and wax flowers under glass domes, and to an admiration for Caravaggio and Gongora. It took me ten years to get over the resulting distaste, not for Proust's works, but for the very idea of reading Proust at all; so unhappily does literary fashion sometimes react on sales-resistant characters (or philistines). Yet the other two vogues were also perfectly genuine and creditable, though characteristically *outré*, expressions of wide and deep movements of taste: the one, the reaction against the Edwardian reaction against the Victorians, the other the reaction against Ruskin's reaction against baroque architecture and painting.

Amongst the Cambridge book-collectors of that distant period the one clearly marked fashion that I recall was for books printed by John Baskerville. This derived from an earlier local devotion to that great English printer which had given his name to a bibliophile society in the University; and although the Baskerville Club had ceased to exist for a decade, a special fondness for Baskerville books (fostered by Maynard Keynes and catered to at old David's bookstall in the Market Place) was still noticeable among the budding bibliophiles. This was a local fashion, differing only in its origin and direction from many another, based more usually on local piety. Yet that Cambridge partiality for an eighteenth-century Birmingham printer illustrates very simply one of the main formative elements in bibliophile (and other) fashions: the influence on one book-collector of others around him. The strongly-marked predilection for William Blake in Glasgow in the eighteen-eighties and in Philadelphia during the past quarter of a century has been due to no discoverable natural affinity. Parts of Glasgow, certainly, now as then, resemble only too closely those dark Satanic mills, and I am told that the same might be said of parts of Philadelphia; but in neither city are these the sections inhabited by the Blake collectors. It was rather the emulative contagion spread among their neighbours by the pioneers and influential enthusiasts—the Bernard B. MacGeorges or the A. Edward Newtons.

There are innumerable examples of this sort of influence in the history of bibliophily. The styles of binding affected by Grolier or Mahieu found countless imitators. The third Duke of Roxburghe coloured the thinking of one generation of book-collectors, Locker-Lampson of another. Buxton Forman made the Romantics fashionable and T. J. Wise the "modern firsts" of the nineteenth century. The consuming passion for three-deckers of a Parrish or a Sadleir has been felt thousands of miles from Pine Valley and Oakley Green. Indeed, the influence of eminent collectors on the general evolution of collecting taste, and their responsibility (whether witting or unwitting) for periodic fashions, are a commonplace of the historians: so much so that the analyst today may find himself more interested in the occasional exceptions to the rule. Mr. W. S. Lewis, for instance, whose enthusiasm for Horace Walpole is a byword in more than two continents, might have been expected to stimulate an increased attention to his hero in other collectors. In fact, however, his activities have had, if anything, the opposite effect.[1]

Fashions, in book-collecting as in other forms of collecting, can often be identified as the excrescences of a movement of taste, the mannerisms of an authentic style, the adoption by imitators of some perhaps legitimate quiddity of a great collector. The Roxburghe-Spencer-Dibdin type of bibliophily, with its concentration on early printing and early illustration, threw off as by-products the indiscriminate craze for Aldines, the elevation of a tall Elzevir (most of the Elzevirs being dumpy little books) to a pinnacle of esteem, and all the other fashions of a century or so ago which now seem to us fads and fetishes. The zeal for Americana of James Lenox and John Carter Brown and the other giants of mid-century collecting in America bade fair for a time to swamp any more general development. The importance attached by the Forman-Wise school to the minor and ephemeral products of their chosen authors produced a sort of pamphlet-mania in the closing years of the century. As for more recent times, the twenties and (by contrast) the thirties would provide a series of fever-charts sufficient to illustrate a whole treatise on fashions in book-collecting. The boom period, which culminated in 1929, is often quoted as a warning against the tendency in collectors of "moderns" to move in undiscriminating herds; and justly so, for the prices paid for many first editions of Barrie, Galsworthy and Shaw, to name only three of the authors then fashionable, were

[1] See p. 51.

ridiculous. Yet the giddy temper of the time was even more injurious to another and much more important development: the long overdue invasion by collectors at large of the literature of the eighteenth century. For this serious and authentic evolution of taste coincided with a fashion-ridden and speculative tendency in the book market, with the result that many good eighteenth-century books were quickly over-inflated, only to suffer more than their share of deflation in the following decade.

Experienced collectors may set fashions. Specialist collectors, subject-collectors, one-author-collectors and just plain hard-headed individualists are usually more or less immune to them. But the desultory collector and the man who likes a change; still more the eager novice, and the book-buyer who has hardly yet dared to admit, even to himself, that he *is* a collector—these are all susceptible creatures: susceptible primarily and properly, no doubt, to the general atmosphere of contemporary collecting *taste*; but also, and more impulsively, susceptible to current *fashions*, as exhibited not only on the shelves and in the talk of their fellow-collectors but also in the bookshops and in booksellers' catalogues. For the influence, on any but the most hard-bitten collector, of booksellers' catalogues, the arrangement of their stock, the direction of their talk over books with a customer, is unquestionably much more powerful than most of them realize.

It was a bookseller, the late great A. W. Evans (of Elkin Mathews Ltd), who observed that "one of the most inexplicable things about collecting is the way it follows fashion." He also maintained that "the collector who fares best in the long run is the man who disregards these fashions." Since he was writing in 1930, his verdict was particularly timely; for fashions, whether deliberately fostered or of the simple self-propelling type, catch on most easily and flourish most widely in times of brisk collecting activity, such as the twenties had certainly been. In such conditions there is usually a crop of new and therefore malleable collectors, as well as an optimistic, an experimental—and possibly also a speculative—spirit amongst the old ones.

That particular fashions in book-collecting often become herd-movements is only partly due to the enthusiasms of the dangerously docile novice. A considerable part is played by another kind of collector: the one who would describe himself as an investor but whom others might call a speculator. I am not thinking of those people who put their money into books or manuscripts because they think them better security than stocks and shares. There are a good many of these today on the Continent and a fair number in England, though very few, presumably, in the United States. Their operations can do no good to book-collecting in the long run; but one cannot tell what kind of harm they will do until these "investors" all try to realize. In respect of the sort of books widely collected in the English-speaking countries this prospect must be viewed with apprehension as well as uncertainty; for we are the first generation in history to witness, in Great Britain, an internal flight from the pound.

No: the speculator who influences fashions (rather than simply the general price-level), and thereby influences other collectors, and thereby, again, influences bibliophily as a whole, is the man who bets on the equation between (*a*) the literary or other interest in a book, an author or a category of books; (*b*) the rarity of the article or articles in question; and (*c*) the likelihood that enough collectors—and dealers —will shortly take the same view, or can be persuaded to follow the same lead. This is an old game. It is no less reputable than any other form of speculation, and it is superior in skill and interest to most. But it is a game on which both the real collector and the bookseller need, and have a right, to keep a much sharper eye than on the innocent vagaries or factitious enthusiasms of the ordinary novice. For the speculator, inasmuch as he is an amateur dealer, is a poacher on both sides of the fence; and though he has his rights like any other member of the public, we must never forget the effect his operations exert, or may later exert, on the broad development of book-collecting.

One thoughtful collector, Mr. John Hayward, put this point very clearly in a recent radio broadcast about book-collecting.[1]

It must always [he said] be in the dealer's own best interest, and so in the interest of book-collecting as a whole [an assumption, incidentally, which does honour to the trade] to resist the periodical attempts of opportunists and speculators to operate in the book market. And so it is in every sense his business to prevent his customers from falling victims to first-edition pushers (by analogy to share-pushers) and to their often seductive devices for creating and exploiting false or artificial values in books.

This view of the bookseller's function in regard to fashions and artificially stimulated markets brings us to a question which concerns both collectors and dealers, viz. what part can booksellers themselves properly and usefully play, whether positively, by promoting them, or negatively by curbing them? A. W. Evans, in the passage I have already quoted, regarded fashions, however inevitable, as regrettable, and commended the collector who disregards them. Yet if they really are inevitable, it is perhaps prudent to come to terms with human nature. Surely both authentic collectors and responsible booksellers should do what they can to control what they cannot prevent. This may be an

[1] See *Book Collecting*. Four Broadcast Talks by R. W. Chapman, John Hayward, John Carter, Michael Sadleir. Cambridge, Bowes & Bowes, 1950.

almost daily problem for a popular bookseller; and without infringing the full freedom of taste and decision in the humblest collector, he will probably play his part by continuing to do what good booksellers have always done, which is to give his customers the best advice he can and sell them the best books that they can be induced to want.

Mr. E. P. Goldschmidt, in an earlier lecture in this series, described the influential part played by the great Florentine bookseller Vespasiano in the establishment of high standards in Renaissance book-making. Vespasiano was enabled to do this by persuading a large number of rich but unlettered customers that manuscript volumes designed by him were the hall-mark of culture: that is, by setting a fashion. And since his taste was admirable, the fashion he set had admirable results. In our own day Evans himself, however he might deplore fashions, knew very well how to set them; and since his judgment was as discerning as his knowledge was remarkable, he rescued from undeserved obscurity, and persuaded his customers to take notice of, enough authors and individual books in the course of fifteen years to fill, if the books could now be reassembled, a good-sized catalogue. Most booksellers, I have observed, have fondnesses for this or that particular author or book: many of them have at one time or another tried their hand at "making" a book they believe in and think insufficiently appreciated by others: some of them, by determinedly specializing in, pushing, and promoting some particular line, have lived to see it come into its own among collectors —and be adopted by their competitors. This is the positive side of the bookseller's possible attitude towards fashions in collecting. Its immediate efficacy will depend to some extent on professional skill; but its long-term contribution to book-collecting as a whole will depend entirely on the good judgment of the bookseller who attempts it.

The negative side is not necessarily more important,

but it is certainly more insistent. For whereas most book-sellers are usually too busy to bother with setting fashions, and need do no more than they feel like in encouraging any current fashion which seems a healthy one, they cannot stand entirely aloof from the course of those others—often, in bullish periods, the majority—which strike the more thoughtful among them as probably unhealthy. It is definitely not the business of any dealer to lay down the law to a customer. If a man is eccentric enough to collect something which seems to his bookseller to be artificial, or even absolutely meaningless, the latter will be disposed to say: let him, and more power to him, for he is breaking new ground and putting more books into circulation. But if he is followed by a pack of other collectors who have no ideas of their own, that is another matter. For then the prices in this fashionable area will go up sharply; and when the bookseller's more suggestible customers ask for the same books, he will have to quote them at figures which, however commercially justifiable today, he cannot honestly regard as sound in the long run. Speculators thrive on sharp price-movements, and among them there are bears as well as bulls. Veteran collectors may chance their arm in an unsettled market without provoking their bookseller to shake a warning finger. But the innocent enthusiast bent on doing something silly poses quite a different problem even for the staunchest upholders of the principle of *caveat emptor*. It is sometimes fatally easy to make a little quick profit out of a sucker, and one of the easiest ways is to give him an extra push down the Gadarene slope of some reigning fashion. But most booksellers realize that he will have a sore head in the morning, and it is only a small and pernicious minority that don't care if he does.

If some fashions are set deliberately and with care, like Shorter and Wise's promotion of George Borrow, many more are started by accident. One doubts whether Merle Johnson and Carroll A. Wilson guessed that their devotion to the first printings of famous quotations would inspire so many sedulous imitators. A. Edward Newton, often a conscious propagandist, probably in the end regretted having compiled his list of One Hundred Good Novels: certainly many a bookseller, confronted with requests for all the books on it by collectors to whom it had not occurred to compile their own, has cursed it heartily. Even the classic Grolier list, which dates from 1903, has been extensively misapplied. As for de Ricci's famous *Book-Collector's Guide*, which was a kind of bibliophilic Debrett of its day, the state of mind which it presupposed in its loyal readers was well summed up by A. J. A. Symons's comment on it.

Mr. Seymour de Ricci [he wrote in 1930], who is a man of knowledge, published a *Book-Collector's Guide* giving brief notes on the "two or three thousand British and American books which fashion has decided are the most desirable for the up-to-date collector." Could there be a more pointed, though unconscious, criticism of what is called, with appropriate ugliness, "high-spot" collecting? What is an "up-to-date" collector? As well talk of an "up-to-date" giraffe.

Fashions thus begotten, like those which are stimulated by a bibliography or a literary rediscovery, can at least be traced to their source. More intriguing to the student of bibliophily are those others whose origin is obscure. Only professionals, perhaps, have much concern with the why and wherefore of that melancholy class of books which were once fashionable, which are not any longer, but which dealers go on listing and collectors go on buying, or at least eyeing respectfully, because they once were. This is a sort of dogged aftermath to the flightiness of yesterday. And, indeed, one of the perpetually perplexing features in the book-collecting scene is the precise nature of that faded aura, not of the changing but rather of an inexplicably unchanging kind, which clings to certain books—and even certain authors—without having any visible connection with their reputation among contemporary readers, whether high-browed or low. "So-and-so," one's friends will say or the cataloguers will write, "so-and-so is an esteemed author"; or again, "Such-and-such a book is a collected book." Not, you will observe, an important author or an interesting author, or even a dark horse worth watching. Not a brilliant book, a significant book or even an underestimated book. But collected, esteemed. That is, presumably, esteemed, whether today or in the past, by a body of other, unknown, collectors. This sort of incantation seems to have a mesmeric effect on many book-buyers. Yet it is no more than an appeal to their instinct for conformity to other people's opinions, for it implies that "esteemed" is some sort of label which can be stuck on an article without regard to its character or merits—and a label which is thought never to lose its compulsion, however fly-blown. In the same spirit a group of stockbrokers might decide to call a particular security "gilt-edged," as if it mattered nothing whether the shares represented a sound or an unsound concern. Such a broker would probably not stay in business long. And it is rather touching evidence of the difference (still occasionally overlooked by the primmer pundits) between the rare-book market and the stock market, that both book-collectors and booksellers extend this sort of loyalty even to the most *démodés* of yesterday's favourites.

PART FOUR

Two Footnotes to an Enquiry

THOMAS J. WISE AND HIS FORGERIES[1]

TEN years ago a group of over fifty rare nineteenth-century "first editions" were exposed as frauds. A verdict of forgery against a person or persons unknown was secured, with almost no dissentients, from the reviewers, the experts, the book-collecting world, and such laymen as were interested. The two comparatively junior "attorneys" who presented this case to the public (both of them members of the London rare-book trade) arraigned as an accessory after the fact the eminent and internationally respected book-collector and bibliographer, Thomas J. Wise, who was then still alive (he died in 1937).

Mr. Graham Pollard and I did not, however, accuse Wise of being a witting accessory; nor did we suggest in print that he might actually have been himself the forger, in spite of our private conviction that he was. But during the succeeding decade others have taken a hand in the further investigation of this fascinating, and in its day sensational, case; and since some new evidence bearing on the responsibility for the forgeries is now being put before the public by Miss Fannie Ratchford in her new book, *The Letters of Thomas J. Wise to John Henry Wrenn* (Knopf), it may be opportune not only to comment on that evidence but to supply a few footnotes to the original indictment.

Before proceeding to consider the new evidence and

---

[1] *An Enquiry* was published in 1934. This article was first printed in the *Atlantic Monthly*, Boston, Mass., February 1945. I was then abroad on government service, and it was written without access to my files. One mistake, due to this handicap, has been corrected in the present text.

reconsider the old, it will be well to recall briefly the contents and conclusions of *An Enquiry into the Nature of Certain Nineteenth Century Pamphlets*, as our treatise was with calculated mildness entitled.

This book was a fully documented exposure of a group of more than fifty "first editions" of such eminent authors as Wordsworth, Tennyson, Dickens, Thackeray, the Brownings, Swinburne, George Eliot, William Morris, R. L. Stevenson, and Rudyard Kipling. These items were mostly of the "privately printed" or the "pre-first" pamphlet type. They appeared in all the standard bibliographies and had been generally accepted for upwards of thirty years. Yet, in the light of the evidence assembled, more than thirty of them were shown to be forgeries and the status of the remainder to be open to considerable suspicion. As a result of our *Enquiry*, the pamphlets have all been reclassified in the British Museum catalogue, whose editors are not prone to sudden enthusiasms.

What put Wise head and shoulders above any other recorded practitioner in fraudulent printing was his early realization (after a few experiments) that *imitations* of books are always discovered: that you must *invent* an edition if you are to avoid the ultimately fatal comparison with a genuine original. Wise was not a forger in the literary sense, like Chatterton or Ireland or the several fabricators of the lost books of Livy. His formula, as simple as it was effective, consisted in taking some suitable piece from a published volume, printing it in pamphlet form with an earlier date, and thus *creating* a first edition for the collectors' market.

So long as he was careful to print from the logical text; if the format and imprint were appropriate; if the hypothetical circumstances of publication and the position in its author's bibliography were plausible; and if he could then get his product on to the right shelves and into the right reference books, it was possible, as Wise proved in spite of mistakes, to get away with murder. His wide-ranging operations were finally unmasked only by the application to each pamphlet of such technical tests of its type-design and paper-content as were hardly to be anticipated in the 1890's, the decade of his main activity as a forger.

In 1934 we could not prove that Wise, who promoted, established and marketed the forgeries, was also their actual creator. It was for this reason, and not from fear of the libel laws, as has been mistakenly or disparagingly suggested, that we did not accuse him of full responsibility. But any candidate for the honour had to pass a series of tests:

1. The forger must have had a large and regular account, and preferably an account of a special character (for example, type-facsimile reprints), at Clay's, who had been proved to have printed the forgeries and had admitted it. Wise had such an account, as did no one else connected with the forgeries.

2. Proof sheets, being rather special items, usually have a traceable origin. If they could be completely and correctly traced for one or more of the forgeries, they must lead back to the forger. Proof sheets of several in fact were located and they all derived from Wise. He had supplied them with bogus pedigrees when selling them.

3. The forger must originally have possessed all the copies of all the forgeries. Therefore, while possession of a single copy of one of them had no significance, and possession of a dozen very little, the greater the number and (more importantly) *the greater the number of each* that were found together, the nearer we were to their original source.

Possession of a long run of titles might indicate nothing more than the owner's keenness on nineteenth-century first editions—there were twenty-four in the Lapham sale in New York in 1908, and Mr. John H. Wrenn owned a complete set; the British Museum possessed twenty-eight, and the Widener Library twenty-five or more. But the only people who had the forgeries in wholesale quantities were Herbert Gorfin and Thomas J. Wise. Gorfin was first Wise's office boy and then Wise's agent in his extensive rare-book dealing, before setting up in business for himself; and he had documentary evidence of the purchase of his holdings from Wise.

So quite apart from the cumulative evidence of Wise's vigorous promotion and, when necessary, defence of the forgeries (others helped to promote them), and of his wholesale dealing in them (others had them in duplicate and sold them, including dealers of the highest repute), there seemed to us no reasonable doubt that the man who passed those three tests must be the forger. That man was Wise; and his reactions to the exposure, both as first laid before him privately by us, eight months before our book came out, and after its publication, only confirmed our suspicions.

There were many, however, who found it impossible to accept even that breath of suspicion which undoubtedly lingers round the scrupulous phrases of the *Enquiry*. They could not believe that a man of Wise's prestige, eminence, academic honours, and (by that time) affluent circumstances could have done such a thing. They had forgotten, or never knew, that Wise, the substantial merchant, had been a rare-book dealer on the side all his life; that at the time he was laying the foundations of his splendid and expensive library he was earning only £500 a year (with a wife to support) and must have needed money badly; and finally (for I think this contributed to his motive) that aspiring bibliographers thrive on the announcement of new discoveries, of which the forgeries provided the most promising aspirant of his day with about half a dozen a year for a decade.

Wise discontinued production, as far as we know, about the turn of the century. He went out of wholesaling between 1909 and 1912, when he jobbed off to Gorfin, in a series of transactions, the main bulk of his stock. One reason for this move may well have been the decline in bibliophilic popularity of a number of the authors represented in the collection;[1] and indeed the prices at which he cleared his shelves stamp this as a "remaindering" operation.

But even in the 1920's, a West End dealer once told me, you could always get a copy of the bogus "Reading" edition of Mrs. Browning's *Sonnets from the Portuguese* from Wise's stock, by applying through Gorfin. And if Wise discovered that a friend had been taken in by the forgery of *his* forgery of Swinburne's *Dead Love* (1864), which always made him furious, he would give him (or sell him) a copy of the "genuine article." The perpetrator of this ironic trick, who produced an imitation of Wise's bogus original, has never been publicly identified.

Graham Pollard and I placed the full evidence for our exposure before Wise in October 1933, in order to give him the opportunity to make a statement. He preferred to prevaricate to us while making every effort behind the scenes to mend his fences for the forthcoming challenge. Mutual friends of Wise and our publishers warned them, in the friendliest but weightiest way, against putting any confidence in these "wild young men." (Wise was describing us in private correspondence as "sewer rats.") Mr. A. Edward Newton wrote to me of the "horrible shock to those of us who are and for years have been playing this book-collecting game" which he anticipated from "this horrible scandal," in which "one of my oldest friends seems to be implicated." "The man," Mr. Newton continued, "is almost a National figure." And so on.

More significantly, Wise bethought him of Gorfin, with whom he had been out of touch for a decade or more, and nvited him to tea. He did not know that Gorfin had

---

[1] Another, no doubt, was his acquisition of the unpublished Swinburne MSS. from The Pines, which provided him with a profitable, and legal racket in "privately" printed pamphlets for the bibliophile market.

"come clean" to us, and he broke the news, as he supposed, that there was "some talk going on about some wrong things" among the pamphlets of which he had sold Gorfin so large a number twenty years before. He suggested that it would be best for all concerned if he took back whatever Gorfin had left "at their market value," which he estimated at a total of £25. Gorfin did not dare tell Wise that we had already taken down his evidence, but he had enough sense to say he would think over Wise's offer. He came straight to my office, and he was still sweating slightly: Wise was an extremely formidable character, and although Gorfin was free, white, and fifty-five, in that choleric presence he was again the subservient office boy. We advised him to write the truth to Wise if he did not, as he insisted, dare to tell him to his face.

He did so, and the result was electric. A series of telegrams summoned him "immediately" to 25 Heath Drive, where Wise offered to repay his whole original investment (£400, *sixteen times* the previous day's offer) in the now worthless pamphlets, on one condition: that Gorfin would endorse his intended statement that they had all come from Harry Buxton Forman, editor of Shelley and Keats, and a notable book-collector of Wise's period, who died in 1917. Gorfin declined to support this story, which he then heard for the first time, and again left, promising to consider Wise's revised offer.

We advised him to accept it, accompanying his acceptance with a specific repudiation of the Buxton Forman story, which seemed to him (and to us) to be an alibi for which Wise needed any support he could beg, borrow, or in this case buy; and we recommended that he get a lawyer to draft the letter. He did so; and he got the £400 in exchange for his stock of the pamphlets, which Wise's lawyers, Messrs Gedge, subsequently certified were burned in their presence. The repudiation of the Forman origin, however, availed Gorfin little, for Wise, both in interviews and letters to the press, made it his main alibi and cited Gorfin in support of it. This moved Gorfin to an indignant protest in *The Times Literary Supplement* (19 July 1934).

The account which Wise had previously given Gorfin had already been retailed to us, as follows: that a certain agent had in the late 1880's offered to Robson's, antiquarian booksellers of Coventry Street, London, a large bundle of "publishers' waste," or "remainders," deriving, he said, from the Edward Moxon sales (1873 and 1878) and possibly elsewhere; that Robson's had declined the lot but had suggested that Wise, who was known as a specialist in pamphlet first editions, might give him £5 for it: and that Wise had done so, to the great profit of himself and, in a much lesser degree, of Gorfin. In short, Wise's commission agent and the subsequent owner of the remainder stock of the forgeries decisively contradicted the origin which Wise was now endeavouring to establish for them.

The Wise alibi, however, received support from another and perhaps more telling quarter. The letter in *The Times Literary Supplement* to which Gorfin had replied (and to which I shall return in a moment) had been at least partially supported, in respect of the alleged Forman origin, by no other than Maurice Buxton Forman, son of the impugned scholar and bibliophile, and himself a distinguished authority on Keats and the bibliographer of George Meredith. His two letters—one to Wise, quoted in full by him, and the other direct to the editor—did not exactly confirm Wise's story that all the forgeries had derived from Forman; but they supported Wise in general and they described Forman's "salting down" of "remainders," and "swaps" with Wise, in such a way as to indicate a state of affairs that was not inconsistent with Wise's account of the matter.

In May 1934 Wise, on the basis of our disclosure of our case to him six months earlier, had decided to anticipate publication of the *Enquiry* by a dogmatic letter to *The Times Literary Supplement* defending himself against the expected attack in respect of the *Sonnets from the Portuguese*, the most interesting of the forgeries (and the most lucrative, for it had brought as high as $1250 at auction). He had not understood clearly the technical tests of paper and type which we had applied to his productions, and his rebuttal was consequently rather an amateurish affair.

This and the other letter bore Wise's signature. But they had in fact been drafted by Mr. Frederick Page, of the Oxford University Press, who had constituted himself Wise's "counsel for the defence" and who relied for "advice" on two senior officers of that august institution.[1] Mr. Page called on us in July 1934, disclosed his status and his authorship of the letters to the *Literary Supplement*, and demanded to see the affidavits which we had taken care to have Gorfin swear for those statements of his on which we had drawn for some of our evidence.

Since Mr. Page seemed genuinely to believe in Wise's innocence, we told him enough, in addition to what we had printed, to convince him that he and his advisers were making themselves practically accessories after the fact by their assistance to Wise; and we warned him that if the defence persisted in their behind-the-scenes attempts to discredit Gorfin or continued to throw the whole responsibility for the forgeries on Forman *without offering any evidence to support the alibi*, we should be compelled to publish a few such damaging facts as Wise's attempt to suborn Gorfin's testimony.

Mr. Page took these warnings so much to heart and so

[1] As cited by him, Mr. (afterwards Sir) Humphrey Milford and Mr. Charles Williams.

little to head that he wrote Wise a letter not only abandoning his defence but conveying some threats which we did not make and were in no position to have made. He sent us a copy of this letter, and we had to point out its inaccuracy as a report of the interview; for Mr. Page had represented us as pro-Gorfin and pro-Forman, whereas we were in fact only concerned to prevent Mr. Page from assisting Wise to throw the blame, *without citing any evidence*, on one man who was dead and could not defend himself, and to discredit another whom we believed to be, however dubious a character in other respects, innocent of complicity in the forgeries. Mr. Page revised his report. A copy of it was sent to America, where further copies of it were circulated by the recipient. Miss Ratchford quotes it in full in her book and draws a number of misleading conclusions from it.

Wise had also prepared a full-length defence to be printed in the *American Book Collector*, a periodical edited by Mr. Charles Heartman. It is understood that Wise cabled instructions to suppress this "defence" as a result of Mr. Page's representations; but he did not have, or did not exercise, any such control over Mr. Gabriel Wells, the prominent rare-book dealer in New York, who among other activities wrote a pamphlet in his defence called *The Carter-Pollard Disclosures*. This was considered by many to have done considerable disservice to the cause it was intended to support, and ironically enough it put one of its readers on to the track of a crucial piece of evidence against Wise, as we shall see.

Messrs Clay's own opinion as to the identity of the only one of their customers who was in a position to have the forgeries executed at their plant was expressed to us privately; and we did not print it since, besides being private, it was only an opinion. But Mr. Wilfred Partington, in a biographical study of Wise called *Forging*

Ahead (New York, Putnam, 1939),[1] printed a verbatim record of an interview between Wise and Mr. Cecil Clay, communicated to him by Mr. Clay, which included Wise's question: "Can't you say you had nothing to do with these things?" and Mr. Clay's reply: "How can I, when you know we printed them for you?"

An important contribution to the forgeries affair in general was made by Mr. Roland Baughman of the Huntington Library, who discovered two fresh additions to the group.[2] Mr. Baughman found Tennyson's *Becket* (1873) to be printed in the forger's favourite type; but, more significantly, he proved that in 1893 Wise had relapsed into the imprudence of imitating a genuine article. He faked copies of his avowed type-facsimile reprint of the recently discovered and very rare *Alaric at Rome* (1840, Matthew Arnold's first publication) and sold them as originals.

Most of these developments had taken place in 1934. In March 1935 I was invited to the library of Mr. Carl H. Pforzheimer, one of America's foremost book-collectors, and offered the opportunity to inspect a document bearing on the origin of the forgeries, on condition that I should not publish it until its owner gave me permission. Mr. Pforzheimer explained that a reference in Mr. Gabriel Wells's polemical pamphlet to Harry Buxton Forman's authorship of an anonymous article entitled "The Building of the Idylls" (of Tennyson) in *Literary Anecdotes of the Nineteenth Century* (edited by Wise and Robertson Nicoll), which we had mistakenly attributed to Wise, had reminded him that there survived in his possession the corrected proofs of this article, with some manuscript notes attached. These had been sold with the Forman library. The manuscript notes, to which no great attention had previously

---

[1] This was revised and expanded into *Thomas J. Wise in the Original Cloth*, London, Robert Hale, 1946.

[2] *The Huntington Library Bulletin*, No. 9, April 1936 (Harvard University Press, Cambridge, Mass.).

been paid, were found to consist of several letters from Forman, one of the principal contributors to *Literary Anecdotes*, to its editor, Wise. Wise had commented interlinearly on a number of points in these letters and sent them back—hence their presence among Forman's effects, where they had fortunately escaped the notice of Wise and the executors when the library was sold to America.

It was my view, expressed then and on numerous subsequent occasions, that these documents ought to be published, for they threw a very interesting light on the relationship existing between Wise and Forman at a time when, as one of the documents proved, that relationship was particularly important to the elucidation of the chief unsolved problem in the forgeries investigation—namely, their authorship. Mr. Pforzheimer, for reasons which I have never understood, persisted year after year in declining either to publish them himself or to allow anyone else to do so.

Later Miss Ratchford was permitted to inspect the documents; but she also was unable to get leave to cite them. As this article goes to press, Mr. Pforzheimer is understood to be in process of printing them in the form of a brochure, and it is much to be hoped that they may now, after being withheld for ten years, be made available to scholars and students in their entirety.[1]

As I must consider myself bound by the letter of my original undertaking, I cannot divulge the contents of these documents. But it will sufficiently indicate the interest of one of them to say that it convicts Wise in his own handwriting of the responsibility for one of the forgeries and includes Forman in the responsibility. Since the *Enquiry* established the homogeneity of the whole group, confession in respect of one forgery would almost automatically extend to them all, even if the pamphlet named were

[1] See the following article in the present volume.

not, as fortunately it is, one of those printed in the forger's most frequently used fount—the fount peculiar to his printers, Messrs Clay.

The fact of Forman's complicity in the production of at least one of the forgeries is no longer in doubt, but the degree and nature of his complicity in the affair as a whole remain speculative. Strong views on this point have at one time and another been adumbrated by Miss Fannie Ratchford, the well-known Brontë expert and librarian of the University of Texas Rare Book Collections. These views have now been set forth in full, with a quantity of evidence, inferential and other, to support them, in the long introduction to her book, which is subtitled "A further inquiry into the guilt of certain nineteenth century forgers."

This substantial volume also contains 460 pages of Wise's letters to his best customer, ranging from 20 February 1894, very early in their acquaintance, to 13 May 1911, the day of Wrenn's death, when the two had been close friends for a dozen years. If anyone doubts the extent of Wise's activities as a dealer in rare books, let him watch the man in action here: it is a full and a masterly performance, from which many professionals could glean a tip or two.

As Miss Ratchford points out, Wise on the whole served Wrenn shrewdly and efficiently, and many of her readers will wonder at the curious psychology of the man who could treat a customer and a friend so well 90 per cent of the time and swindle him so thoroughly the other ten per cent. But it is that other ten per cent which is our concern here:[1] for Wise sold Wrenn at various times copies of every one of his forgeries, duplicates of several, and proof sheets of two. And his technique of promoting these sales is both

---

[1] In fact, more like two or three per cent; for though Wise sold Wrenn a number of made-up and otherwise sophisticated books, the forgeries themselves do not, after all, number more than sixty volumes.

fascinating in itself and significant, because it presumably illustrates his methods with his many other customers. He raises expectations and recounts imaginary bargainings; he pulls off gratifying deals with non-existent owners; and he often supplies plausible, but completely bogus, sources—Walter Harrison, "nephew of Moxon," Edward Carpenter, Frederick Crawley (Ruskin's old valet), Mrs. Dykes Campbell, R. H. Horne, Miss Tadema (daughter of the painter), a mysterious and almost certainly fictitious "Dr. Underwood," and several more.

Miss Ratchford, in her Introduction, is naturally at pains to vindicate the main bulk of the Wrenn Library, since 1918 one of the prime ornaments of the library at Austin, from those suspicions which have attached to its contents since Wise, who supplied perhaps three-quarters of the volumes, was exposed in 1934 as, if not actually a forger, at least a careless judge of a book's authenticity.

Miss Ratchford is mainly concerned, however, with a re-examination of the question of the responsibility for the group of forgeries then exposed. She does not dispute Wise's involvement, but she challenges what she rather sweepingly calls "Carter and Pollard's *conviction* [my italics] that the whole burden and range of guilt for the forgeries was encompassed in Thomas J. Wise." Miss Ratchford does not cite any evidence for this conviction except the Frederick Page letter to which I have already referred—and in fact we had, I think, reasonably open minds all along.

But in 1934 we lacked *evidence* against anyone but Wise, and even against him we lacked enough to justify an accusation. Some evidence of possible connivance we subsequently discovered ourselves in respect of Clay's foreman, though it remains circumstantial.[1] The *Literary*

[1] And therefore unpublished.

Anecdotes document provides evidence of complicity against Forman in addition to completing the case against Wise. But it remains for Miss Ratchford to convince her readers, as well as Messrs Carter and Pollard, of the existence of what she calls (on page 77, before she has presented any of her evidence) "the Wise-Forman-Gosse workshop," and of the complicity of Herbert Gorfin.

Miss Ratchford builds up her case against Forman with vigour. She cannot play the ace because Mr. Pforzheimer has it, and has no more allowed her to use it than anyone else; but she knows it is there, and if she can only refer to it in a sad and tantalizing footnote, that knowledge enables her to ruff and finesse elsewhere with a freedom which she may be thought to have exercised rather too enthusiastically. She does, however, make several telling points based on factors which Pollard and I insufficiently appreciated; and even if some of the clues lay in the hitherto locked files of the Wise-Wrenn correspondence, it must none the less be a legitimate satisfaction to Miss Ratchford to be able to establish (albeit with the final proof uncited) what she has long believed—that Forman was implicated.

But she has permitted herself a certain amount of special pleading in her case against him, particularly in respect of the sensibility to similarities or differences in commonplace contemporary type-designs which can legitimately be postulated in the compilers of author-bibliographies and the editors of volumes of poetry (such as Forman). She herself has not apparently appreciated one factor recognized in the *Enquiry*: that in the 1880's and 1890's the same specific founders' types, in the regular 10 and 12 point text sizes, were being used in dozens of printing shops all over England. It is hardly reasonable to accuse Forman of failing to recognize one or another of half a dozen such founts when he saw it again, while she herself argues as if she attached as much guilty significance to founts *common* to Clay and many other printers as to the key hybrid fount which was *peculiar* to Clay.

Many a bibliographer examined the "Reading" *Sonnets* with care, if not with scepticism. But it took the eagle eye of Stanley Morison, the most expert living analyst of type, to perceive for the first time in 1932 the significant features in its type; and it was only by what we described as "a lucky accident" that Pollard and I in 1933 identified that type in an honestly imprinted book and so traced it to its origin. Is it reasonable, then, to take for granted such microscopic discrimination as Miss Ratchford finds it incredible that Forman should not have possessed?

The employment of this sort of special pleading, needless against Forman, whose complicity is certain, cannot but affect our readiness to accept Miss Ratchford's indictments against her other defendants, in respect of whom no such conclusive evidence as the *Literary Anecdotes* document exists. She applies to both Forman and Edmund Gosse (an equally distinguished *littérateur* and an equally keen, though much less accomplished, book-collector) the argument that the inclusion, in their libraries of nineteenth-century first editions, of a substantial number of the forged pamphlets automatically implies a guilty knowledge of their character. "The Buxton Forman Library," Miss Ratchford writes, "contained thirty-two forgeries plus eleven duplicates. . . . Again, as in Gosse's case [Gosse had twenty], this is too large a number for so astute a bibliographer to have held innocently." Yet that reasonably astute institution the British Museum held more than Gosse, the Huntington and University of Texas Libraries more than Forman. Were these also guilty?

Aside from this general, and as I think untenable, inference, Miss Ratchford's case against Gosse rests on two arguments. First is her belief, fortified by that of "a score or more of persons accustomed to judging and identifying handwriting," that the correction *mangoes* for *mangos* in the margin of the proof sheets of the fraudulent E. B. Browning pamphlet *The Runaway Slave at Pilgrim's Point* is in Gosse's hand.

When years ago Miss Ratchford, with the courtesy characteristic of the library at Austin, provided us with photostats of these proofs, we were after careful comparisons "unable to identify" the hand. These photostats are in London; and on learning of Miss Ratchford's identification, I sent a cable to Graham Pollard, asking for a further scrutiny. I transcribe his reply (purged of one or two misprints pardonable in an unbibliographical cable-operator): "Mangoes hand unascribable but more like Wise than Gosse stop letters not Gosse type." Miss Ratchford has reproduced the relevant page in facsimile, with a selection of words from Edmund Gosse's regular handwriting alongside it; but her readers will note that the only professional expert whose opinion was sought (the Chief of the Identification Division of the Texas Department of Public Safety) found the specimens "insufficient and not the proper standards upon which to base an opinion." Yet even if her readers follow Miss Ratchford in seeing a similarity (as I do not), they may think (as I do) that a single word, written in the careful but not always characteristic script normally adopted for proof corrections, in the margin of a book unconnected with Gosse by any other evidence, is an uncommonly slender thread with which to hang a man.

Miss Ratchford's second specific charge against Gosse is that he fathered the story of the printing of Mrs. Browning's *Sonnets*, knowing it to be false, and "deliberately propagated it for the purpose of authenticating the forged pamphlet." She concludes that "Gosse divides the guilt with Wise, in fifty-fifty proportions." Gosse certainly introduced the bogus "first edition" of the *Sonnets* to the world, in 1894; and since he did not list his copy in the 1893 catalogue of his library it is reasonable to suppose that he had only just acquired it. In the *Enquiry* we inclined to the idea that the anonymous informant whom Gosse quoted as his authority for the whole story of Mrs. Browning's coy disclosure of her poems to her husband, of his reactions, and of the subsequent private printing, was Wise himself. But besides misreading some of the evidence then at our disposal, we had been unaware of certain letters written by Gosse in which, in replying to inquiries how the poems could have been printed in 1847 when letters to Browning himself show that they had not been disclosed to him till 1849, Gosse, abandoning the fictitious intermediary, had stated (letter to J. R. Burton, 1927) that he had had "the story regarding the authorship of those poems" direct from Browning himself. If we had known of this evidence, we should have realized, as perhaps we ought to have done anyway, that it was necessary to distinguish two elements in Gosse's story, first printed in 1894, but best known in *Critical Kit-Kats*, 1896: first, the major part, the picturesque account of wife and husband and the love poems; second, the brief passage giving particulars of the alleged "Reading" edition.

The first element, except for some differences of detail, is confirmed by several other accounts deriving directly from Robert Browning. The second element, being false, must have come from some other source. We thought, and I still think, it came from Wise, with a copy of the book (at a bargain price, no doubt) to provide ocular evidence; and was incorporated by Gosse in his main story without that "most careful investigation and certain proof" to which Miss Ratchford justly thinks he was "obligated" but which was not in fact characteristic of Gosse's work either as biographer or critic. I think Gosse was gulled by Wise, as I think he was in the matter of Swinburne's *Dolores* (see

Enquiry, page 273), which Miss Ratchford, rather surprisingly, does not cite. I think that in later years, when he was cross-questioned by Lilian Whiting and J. R. Burton, he realized there was something seriously wrong with the book,[1] and that he took the line of least resistance, brushing off his questioners with a rather high-handed statement of half-truths. Gosse defends (with perfect justice) "the story of the *authorship* of those poems" (my italics): he says nothing about their printing as the "Reading" *Sonnets*.

This must remain a question for the jury, and lack of space may have caused me to do some injustice to Miss Ratchford's argument in respect of this particular book. Though she does not cite any evidence for his connection with any other specific forgery, yet with her reference to the "Wise-Forman-Gosse workshop" and her inferences from Gosse's holdings of the group of forgeries and the sum they netted him when his library was sold, she lines him up against the wall as a full-dress fellow-conspirator. I propose, therefore, to put in evidence two letters: one from Wise to Gosse about selling him some of the forgeries; the other from Gosse to Wise acknowledging the gift of another forgery. The first is inserted in Gosse's copy of George Eliot's *Brother and Sister*, one of the forgeries, and is dated "Mon. 19th [no month] 1896."

My dear Gosse,

Thanks for yours. I am so glad the little books please you. You shall most certainly have the "Agatha" [*by George Eliot—a forgery*] as soon as I can find it. It is generally understood and I think rightly, that 25 copies of "Brother and Sister" [*another forgery*] were printed—as there were of "Agatha"—But I have no absolutely certain and unquestionable evidence to go on as I have in the case of "Agatha."

[1] Since I wrote this in 1945, it must stand. But on further reflection I am not sure that these letters necessarily imply even that at this later date Gosse had become suspicious of the book. The mere fact of having been caught out in an inaccuracy about dates might well account for his autocratic handling of the snipers.

It may interest you to know that the copy of "Leoni" [*by Ruskin—a forgery*] I sent you was formerly the property of Fredk. Crawley, Mr. Ruskin's old factotum, now living at Oxford upon a pension of £100 a year allowed him from Brantwood. I looked him up in 1889 when I was hunting all round for material for my Ruskin Bibliography. I bought from him all the relics he had—books, letters, sketches, among other things this tract.

Forgive this haste.

Yours,
T. J. WISE.

The second letter came from the library of H. T. Butler, a friend of Wise, which was sold in 1934, and it was very kindly transcribed for me by its subsequent owner, Mr. Robert Metzdorf. It is dated from 17 Hanover Terrace, London, 27/10/09.

How generous and kind of you, my dear Wise, to give me this beautiful copy of the 1867 "Dolores" [*by Swinburne—a forgery*]. I am very grateful to you.

Have you ever solved the mystery of its production? I have very minutely collated it with the text of 1866, and there are three extremely trifling variations. All three are errors in 1867 where 1866 was correct. I wonder whether Hotten [*the publisher of* Poems and Ballads (1866), *whose imprint was quite plausibly used on the title-page of the forgery* (1867)] had any secret object in this production? Why he did it, in fact? It would be interesting to try and work out the causes of the reprint, which I suppose, from its present rarity, was very limited. . . .

Yours sincerely,
EDMUND GOSSE.

I will ask the impartial reader of these letters, which have only been preserved by accident and can hardly be supposed written "for the record," whether they read like those which fellow-conspirators would exchange about the fruits of their conspiracy. If Gosse was a partner in the "workshop," why does he write in 1909 like a delighted amateur to a benevolent professional? Why is he treated in 1896—the very year in which, according to Miss Ratchford, he was knowingly promoting one of the group—to a "promotion and sales" letter which is the spitting image, in tone and tactics, of a score of those printed by Miss Ratchford to illustrate Wise's technique when selling forgeries to Wrenn?

The remaining object of Miss Ratchford's accusations is the late Herbert Gorfin, who has been referred to already in this article. Gorfin, who was Wise's office boy in the essential oil business and his agent and factotum in much of his book-dealing, must have known very well that Wise was up to all the tricks of the trade (and to many which the antiquarian book trade at least would indignantly spurn). He himself acted as Wise's "front" in deals with Wrenn and many another—at Wise's office he was "Herbert," and when Wise was writing to Wrenn in Chicago to offer a bargain he became "Gorfin, a small bookseller of Hither Green"—where, indeed, he operated a small mail-order business from his home address.

But there is a wide gap between lending oneself to shady deals and conspiracy to forge. Pollard and I, who had the advantage of confronting Gorfin in person with the facts, cross-questioning him, and putting him through his evidence on oath, concluded that he did not know the pamphlets were forgeries. He was ten years old when the earliest appeared, and twenty-one when the last that we know of was produced (1899). Miss Ratchford believes that he must have known, then or later, what they were; but beyond general inferences of probability she adduces only one piece of evidence against him.

That evidence is a receipt purporting to be signed by Walter Harrison ("Moxon's nephew") and accompanying a copy of the fraudulent Tennyson's *Morte D'Arthur* (1842) sold by Wise to Wrenn, which Miss Ratchford believes was written by Gorfin, using a sharp pen to disguise his hand. She reproduces this document in facsimile, along with other examples of undoubted Gorfin script, and I dare say most of her readers will concur in her identification. But Wise provided bogus origins for many other books he sold besides the forgeries, and Gorfin certainly knew it. So that even if the writing were agreed to be his, it would not necessarily imply a knowledge that this particular book was a forgery, or do anything to promote Gorfin from his present grade of jackal into that of fellow-conspirator.

In conclusion: the Pforzheimer document will be seen, when its owner finally publishes it,[1] to be a cardinal addition to the evidence in the forgeries affair. It is highly satisfactory that Wise left, in his own hand, even summary evidence of his guilt; and the inclusion of Forman in that short but sufficient sentence confirms some at least of the suspicions which Miss Ratchford has long held and which she has so amply expounded in her book. But if that document had been published in Wise's lifetime, it might, conceivably, have extorted a full confession from him. And at the least it must have elicited *some* statement, *some* addition, from the best possible authority, to the story of the most ingeniously conceived, the best executed, and the most successful fraud in the history of book-collecting.

Meanwhile Miss Ratchford has reopened the whole case with some new evidence and a salvo of new accusations. I am not myself convinced by all her deductions; and in the complicity of Forman there remains much uncertainty as to its degree and its extent. But even if her readers now conclude, or further discoveries should suggest, that the forgeries were the work of a ring, I shall be much surprised if Thomas J. Wise has to be dethroned from his commanding position as the master mind.

[1] See the next article.

THOMAS J. WISE AND
H. BUXTON FORMAN [1]

by John Carter and Graham Pollard

TWELVE years ago, in *An Enquiry into the Nature of Certain Nineteenth Century Pamphlets*, we offered evidence that thirty esteemed and reputedly rare Victorian "first editions" were forgeries and that a number more were open to varying degrees of suspicion. Plenty of minor errors in our work have since come to light: but its main contentions have not been seriously challenged, and the pamphlets concerned have now been reclassified in the British Museum catalogue.

The *Enquiry* could not hope, and did not pretend, to have identified all the members of what it showed to have been a homogeneous group of forgeries, all (after a few experimental efforts) conforming to a single, though subtly varied, formula and all almost certainly coming from the same printing house. Our own further investigations have satisfied us that the four Swinburne pamphlets which bear the (bogus) imprint of "Charles Ottley, Landon, & Co.," are members of the group, and details will be published in due course. [2] Meanwhile independent research in the Huntington Library (owning fifty-four out of the fifty-five books on our list) and in the Wrenn Library at the University of Texas (owning all fifty-five, plus original proofs of two) resulted in the exposure of three further pamphlets, two by Tennyson and one by Matthew Arnold. In the years after 1934, however, it was evident, as Mr. Baughman wrote in No. 9 of the *Huntington Library Bulletin*, "that attention was being focused on personalities rather than on

---

[1] This article was first published, signed, in *The Times Literary Supplement* of 1 June 1946. The *Enquiry* was published in 1934.

[2] *The Firm of Charles Ottley, Landon & Co., Footnote to an Enquiry.* Loudon, Hart-Davis; New York, Scribners, 1948.

the crucial evidence in the case," and in fact his own paper has been almost the only serious contribution on the technical side.

The question of the forger's identity had, of course, been examined in the *Enquiry*. But we were compelled to admit that "this part of our investigation has led to no conclusive result." In a matter of such gravity it was obvious that no identification could be attempted without proof, and we had no proof. For on the evidence available to us in 1934 the conjecture that Wise was the forger was no more than the most plausible of several unverifiable hypotheses. It is true that his reaction to the exposure did little to reduce the degree of suspicion which inevitably attached to him as the principal bibliographical sponsor of the forgeries. The only known proof-sheets of any of them came from him. He was the only wholesale source of supply, and if the forgeries were made for money it was Wise who collected it. He alone commanded the confidence of their printers, R. Clay and Sons. Although none of their ledgers from before 1911 survives, the forger's account must have been substantial: one to be remembered, if not for its nature, at least for its size. Messrs Clay did not remember doing business with Forman or Gosse or Gorfin; but they did with Wise.

Wise's only coherent line of defence was the statement that any of the pamphlets which he had ever possessed (contrary to various earlier statements in print) had come to him from Harry Buxton Forman, the editor of Shelley and Keats, a notable collector in his day and a close friend of Wise's. H. B. Forman had then been dead for nearly twenty years. "I was only the vehicle," Wise was reported to have informed a London newspaper; "I was the messenger lad who took the goods for delivery. They were planted on Forman, and not on me." In solitary substantiation of this defence he cited, in this *Supplement*, an ambiguous but rather disquieting letter written (at his insistence) by Mr. Maurice Buxton Forman; though at the same time he tried unsuccessfully, first by threats and then by bribery, to induce Mr. Herbert Gorfin, who had been *his* "messenger lad" in his many years of book-dealing, to testify that the forgeries came from Forman, not from himself. Wise offered no other explanation and no shred of documentary evidence in support of his allegation. In face of the powerful array of evidence against him it was not surprising that this sudden change of front was received with scepticism.

There was, however, in existence in 1934 a piece of paper, written on in 1896, which would have enabled us to write the missing chapter to *An Enquiry*—"The Forger Identified." It would also have provided Wise with what his critics demanded—documentary evidence of Forman's complicity in the fraud: though only at the expense oi convicting himself at the same time.

This letter is reproduced in a book[1] recently published in America, and its contents are here transcribed, with their surrounding context. The main text is in Forman's hand: Wise's interlinear comments are square-bracketed and introduced with his initials. "Mrs. Severn" was no doubt Mrs. Arthur Severn, Ruskin's cousin and literary executrix; and the volume which provoked Forman's protest must have been *Letters from John Ruskin to Rev. F. A. Malleson*, 1896—one of a series of "privately printed" booklets produced by Wise for sale to bibliophiles. Most of these bore the imprint of his Ashley library, and they were listed in a little catalogue, revised from time to time, to which Forman refers in his final sentence.

---

[1] *Between the Lines*. Letters and Memoranda interchanged by H. Buxton Forman and Thomas J. Wise. With a Foreword by Carl H. Pforzheimer and an introductory essay and notes by Fannie E. Ratchford. University of Texas Press. 1945.

Certificates

As to certificates, thanks for your long story about Mrs. Severn
—with whom you *do* seem to have put yourself in a difficulty.
There is more than "an appearance of dishonesty." [T. J. W.,
who underlines Forman's *dishonesty*—How can there be *"dishonesty"* when she is not *deprived* of anything?] The appearance
is this—that you are reluctant to say how many are printed;
& say "a few" because some will understand that to mean 3 or
4, some 10 or 12, some 20 or 30, & so on. [T. J. W.—"A few"
MEANS (*heavily underlined*) "a few," & can mean nothing else!]
There cannot on the face of it be an honest reason for wanting
the number printed to be differently conjectured by different
people; and it turns out that the appearance is borne out by the
fact that, printing 30 (more or less), you want some one to think
you only print 10 or 12. [T. J. W.—Quite so. And we print
"Last Tournament" in 1896, & want "someone to think" it was
printed in 1871! *The moral position is exactly the same!* But
there is no "dishonesty." Mrs. Severn does not *buy* her copy
under the impression that only 10 or 12 are printed: I *give* it
to her *gratis*!] However, that is all your affair; and I have done
on it, so far as your Ruskin Letters go. But what has that to
do with Browning Letters? As to the "Ashley List," it does
not affect the question—has absolutely no bearing upon it.
[T. J. W. *replies, promising numbered certificates in future.*]

The crucial passage is Wise's retort beginning "Quite
so." This reference to the printing of Tennyson's "The
Last Tournament" (falsely dated 1871, and already proved
a forgery on the triple grounds of type, paper and text)
is not endorsed by Forman, and we have therefore,
strictly speaking, still only Wise's word for Forman's
complicity. But if the context and tone carry to most
readers the conviction they carry to us, this is indis-
putable evidence (*a*) that Wise and Forman both had a
share in the forgery of "The Last Tournament" and (*b*)
that this was done with a commercial motive, and not (as
has by some been supposed of the whole group) as part of
an elaborate joke.

It is eminently satisfactory that Wise is, at last, convicted;

and out of his own mouth. But if this evidence is, as it certainly is, extremely important, it is still necessary to be careful in extracting inferences from it. Just as in 1934 Wise's unsupported (and therefore, as many thought, disgraceful) aspersions against Forman caused the then available evidence against him to be discounted, so now there may be some inclination to swing to the opposite extreme and, on the strength of a *prima facie* probability, roundly to proclaim Forman as Wise's fellow-conspirator in the whole complex scheme, involving over fifty pamphlets, which had been in operation for at least eight years before the date of this document and continued for at least three thereafter. Wise's brief revelation—and there is no other reference to the forgeries *as such* among these papers—does not exclude the possibility of a prolonged conspiracy, nor the possibility of a wider conspiracy than two persons (Miss Ratchford's accusations against Gosse and others will be remembered): but it does not support either. It gives no hint of the proportion of responsibility between the two men, even over this one book; nor indeed is it likely that any written evidence exists—or ever existed— which would reveal to us who was the prime mover, who the accomplice, in the fraud, or for how long. It will not be forgotten that a mass of circumstantial evidence has already established Wise as the production manager and chief salesman. If it be conceded that joint responsibility for one forgery justifies the presumption of at least joint knowledge of others, it will be for consideration whether (*a*) the original conception was Forman's, with Wise as his executive agent, or (*b*) Wise was the main organizer as well as the executive, with Forman as his editorial adviser and assistant promoter, or (*c*) these two were not the only conspirators. The arguments for these hypotheses are too long to summarize here; but in our opinion the new evidence is not, in itself, decisive between them.

Whatever view of this question may prevail, it will be recognized as a piece of remarkable good fortune that there has survived even a single piece of written evidence of a conspiracy which must surely have been organized and operated by word of mouth. That Wise should have been galled by Forman's criticisms into the fatally revealing rejoinder was human, however imprudent; that the result should have been preserved is almost a miracle. The document is one of a number of manuscripts all having to do with *Literary Anecdotes of the Nineteenth Century*, two volumes (of a projected ten) published in 1895–96 under the editorship of W. Robertson Nicoll (inactive) and Wise, to which Forman was a substantial contributor. These were included, with the manuscript, galley and page proofs of Forman's article "The Building of the Idylls," in the sale of his library (Oct. 7, 1920, lot 1204); and they subsequently passed into the collection of Mr. Carl H. Pforzheimer, of New York. They were recalled to their owner's attention in 1934 by a passage (correcting one of our errors) in Mr. Gabriel Wells's pamphlet in defence of Wise, and the significance of the document now published was immediately appreciated. It was shown, in confidence, to one of us in the spring of 1935; but Mr. Pforzheimer, in spite of repeated representations, continued for nearly a decade unwilling to publish it. It must therefore remain a matter of opinion whether its publication before Wise's death in 1937 might not have extracted a full, or even a partial, confession; but it is hardly conceivable that he could have ignored it entirely, and some—perhaps much —vital information about the forgeries (identified and unidentified) has thus been lost.

But if Mr. Pforzheimer, by an exercise of the right of property, has withheld evidence from the public too long, his belated decision to publish it will none the less be widely welcomed—or as widely as 525 copies at $8 apiece allows. And it was eminently appropriate that Miss Fannie Ratchford should be asked to introduce and annotate this selection from the main body of proofs and MSS. For Miss Ratchford has long believed Forman guilty, and she is now proved right. In the introduction to her edition of Wise's letters to his best customer, John H. Wrenn,[1] she built up a voluminous case against him—a case wanting its full conviction from her inability to cite the evidence now published, which she also had been allowed to see but not to use. In her introduction here she continues to pursue Forman, to the almost total eclipse of Wise; and the latter actually emerges from this book as a rather plaintive figure.

The illustrations, which quite needlessly include the title-page and binding of *Literary Anecdotes*, are very clearly reproduced, but the reader is not so well served by the editor's transcriptions. Her typographical formula for distinguishing Forman's MS. from Wise's precludes consistent indication of the frequent and characteristically emphatic underlining and also obscures the sense where Wise has underlined Forman as a *point d'appui* for a note. Apart from this confusion, moreover, any reader who compares the text with the plates will notice more than a dozen mistakes in transcription: a piece of inattention unexpected in the product of a well-known library and of a university press. But these are trivial blemishes on a book which does at last dissipate some of the cloud of suspicion about the origin of the forgeries and provides a firm basis for further research. For this notable step forward many besides ourselves have cause to be grateful to Mr. Pforzheimer and Miss Ratchford.

[1] *See the preceding article in this book.*

PART FIVE

One Bibliographical Sermon

NINETEENTH-CENTURY ENGLISH BOOKS: SOME BIBLIOGRAPHICAL AGENDA[1]

IT is a distasteful fact, but a fact, that bibliographical technique for dealing with nineteenth-century books as physical objects is still at a rudimentary stage of development. It is my contention that we can no longer afford to let its development continue haphazard, uncoordinated, and piecemeal.

To understand why nineteenth-century bibliography is complicated, one need only look at the list of those innovations in the manufacture of books which marked the industrial revolution in our particular field. Let me remind you of a few of the most significant:[2]

1800 Senefelder's English patent for the invention of lithography.

1800 Stanhope's iron printing press under test at Bulmer's.

1803 The "Fourdrinier" cylindrical paper-making plant, for endless web production, completed by Gamble and Donkin.

1804 The first book printed by Stanhope's stereotype process: the commercially practicable development of Ged's invention of 1739 and Firmin Didot's experiments of 1795.

1811 Koenig patents the steam-powered press.

1822 The first type-composing machine patented by Church.

1823 First confirmed use of cloth for edition-binding.

[1] The Windsor Lecture, delivered at the University of Illinois in 1951.
[2] Mostly drawn from the much fuller list in David Greenhood and Helen Gentry's *Chronology of Books and Printing* (New York, 1936).

1826 First photo-engraving on a metal plate, by Niepce, Daguerre's partner.

1832 The "Imperial" Arming-press, and Leighton's process for direct gilt-blocking on cloth.

1837/9 Electrotyping (Jacobi, St. Petersburg; Spencer, Liverpool; Adams, New York).

1848 Applegath's invention of the rotary printing press.

The second half of the century saw the introduction, in the field of illustration, of collotype, photo-etched line-blocks, half-tone, photogravure, and the three-colour process; and in the field of typesetting, of the linotype (Mergenthaler, 1886) and monotype (Lanston, 1887) machines.

It is a commonplace that the nineteenth century produced more radical changes in book production than the whole previous history of printing since Gutenberg. It is not always realized that its first thirty-five years alone were more revolutionary than the preceding 350. Nor was this transformation confined to manufacture. Changes in the structure of the book itself were matched by, and closely connected with, changes in the reading habits of the public, and changes—more directly significant for the bibliographer—in the articulation of the distributive trades. For it was during the decade or two on each side of 1800 that the division between bookseller and publisher was effectively established. Booksellers, indeed, continued to act occasionally as publishers; some publishers continued, especially for the export market and in the handling of fiction, to act as wholesale booksellers (or, as Americans call them, jobbers). But the specialization of function in the English trade developed far more rapidly and far more thoroughly than in America, where to this day one firm (which shall be nameless),[1] operates a printing house, a bindery, a publishing business, a subscription book business, a retail bookstore and a rare book department.

[1] This was Charles Scribner's Sons, by whom I was then employed. The statement is no longer accurate.

If it had not been for William Pickering's consciousness of the separate function and enlarged responsibility of the publisher, we might never have had edition-binding in cloth. If it had not been for the prodigious appetite for reading and for information which sprang from the increase in literacy, and drew its yeast from the ferment of the industrial revolution, expansionist publishers of the second quarter of the century—Constable, Murray, Bentley, Chambers—would not have found public support for the ambitious programme of good, cheap books which the new technology made possible and which changed the face of English publishing. To the social and the literary historian these are matters for congratulation. But the physical results have presented the bibliographer with problems quite different from those of the hand-press age, and no less intrinsically baffling. That these problems are in practice even more baffling to most of us is due to their having been largely neglected by the guides and philosophers in whom, for earlier books, we have learned to place our confidence. In their classic paper, *Some Points in Bibliographical Description*,[1] Pollard and Greg summed up thus the attitude of the hierarchy in the first decade of the present century: "Here, happily," they said, "we are only concerned with the practice of our early printers, and are therefore able to avoid the apparently hopeless confusion which has resulted from modern trade methods and the introduction of stereotyping."

Two examples may serve to indicate the effect of this "happy avoidance" of "apparently hopeless confusion." Falconer Madan's memorandum on *Degressive Bibliography*, which was appended to Pollard and Greg's paper, proposed four formulae for the bibliographical description

[1] Delivered in 1906; published in the *Transactions of the Bibliographica Society*, IX, 1908.

of a book. Form A was "a full description"; Form B, "a description adapted for books of the seventeenth century"; Form D, "a minimum description for a mere list of works" —i.e., a hand-list or finding-list. The one that concerns us here is his Form C: "a short description such as befits modern literature," which by implication meant, to Madan and his confrères, any book published after 1700. He gives an example of Form C, as applied to a book of 1908; and, as Michael Sadleir recently noted (with an almost inhuman restraint from comment),

the presence of sixteen illustrations is recorded, but not their placing nor the manner of their reproduction; a publisher's (inset) catalogue is recorded at the end, and actually included in the collation (though certainly not on text paper); but no date is given, although the only interest of any inset catalogue is to distinguish a later from an earlier binding-up. The actual binding of the book is not mentioned at all.[1]

This was the measure of a good STC man's opinion of "modern books" forty years ago; and it is an opinion by no means extinct today.

A second example is provided by the definition given to the term *edition* by two such formidable authorities as the *Oxford English Dictionary* and the late R. B. McKerrow, whose *Introduction to Bibliography for Literary Students* remains, and will surely always remain, the standard treatise on its subject. An edition, in their view, comprises the whole number of copies of a work printed at any time from one setting of type, including copies printed from stereotype, electrotype or any other kind of plates made from that type. Unlike some of those who have had to apply it to modern books, I have no quarrel with this definition; for there are adequate terms for the subdivisions of an edition. But anyone who uses the words *first edition* or *original edition* in describing a modern book needs to re-

[1] The Bibliographical Society's *Studies in Retrospect* 1945, p. 149n.

member that they include a good deal more than McKerrow ever bargained for. No matter how many later impressions, later editions, corrected reissues, remainder bindings and the like may have succeeded the first impression of the first edition, that edition has a continuing existence as long as type or plates remain from which it could be reprinted. Moreover, duplicate plates may have been made for printing from at different times, in different places, even in different countries; and the products of these are inalienable units of the first edition. Furthermore, as Professor Bowers has pointed out,[1] a first edition can nowadays survive—*in posse* if not *in esse*—even the destruction of the original type *and* plates. For he admits, however reluctantly, that the punched ribbon produced by the monotype keyboard operator, when fed again into the caster, would in theory produce a type-setting indistinguishable from the original one; the printed products of which, having the same origin, belong to the same edition as those copies printed from the first casting. And he is not prepared to exclude entirely from a similar state of grace copies of a book produced by the photolithographic offset process, which can be put into operation without type, plates or monotype roll, simply from one surviving example of the original edition.

If I now digress for a moment to consider why nineteenth-century bibliography has not been taken seriously by our mentors in the past, it is not by way of post-mortem (for the patient is very much alive), but because diagnosis must precede even the most tentative prescription. Mr. Sadleir, I think, put his finger on the two main reasons, in an essay contributed to the Bibliographical Society's *Studies in Retrospect*, where he had the ungrateful task of explaining why the Society had paid during the first fifty years of its life practically no attention whatever

---

[1] *Principles of Bibliographical Description*, 1949, p. 381.

to the bibliography of nineteenth-century books. The first reason was the natural preoccupation of the fathers of modern bibliography—such men as Bradshaw, Proctor, Pollard, McKerrow and Greg, to name only my own countrymen—with "the products of early periods in the history of printing, when standardization hardly existed, whence few if any records survived, and when the material for study was definitely international rather than national." Even when much of the emphasis was transferred from incunabula to the Elizabethans, Restoration and Augustan literature continued to be ignored. As for the Romantics, and the Regency novelists, and the Victorians, they remained in outer darkness. The average nineteenth-century book, indeed, was by STC standards not even rare; so that if and when later students might need to tackle them, it was taken for granted that plenty of copies would be available.

In the sense that this was putting first things first, we should surely agree with Mr. Sadleir's conclusion that such an attitude was "inevitable and logical." Unless, however, we are to resign ourselves to waiting for authoritative attention to nineteenth-century bibliography until every *t* has been crossed and every *i* dotted for the previous centuries, we must also take account, in the hope of correcting it, of Mr. Sadleir's second reason for this sustained neglect. "This reason," he observed, "is more complicated, and has its origin in the suspicion of the book-collector which was until lately deeply ingrained in the minds of scholars and librarians. For it was among collectors that nineteenth-century books first came to the front."

This is true; and it is greatly to the credit of book-collectors that it should have been so, even if Mr. Sadleir, doyen of nineteenth-century bibliophiles today, is too delicate to say so. Yet the fact had unfortunate consequences for bibliography. Book-collecting has always sported a lunatic fringe, and from time to time it has suffered also from speculative elements. The antics of both parties (and, let me be the first to say, of the booksellers who encouraged or connived at those antics) were nicely calculated to discourage serious-minded scholars from just the sort of serious-minded scholarship which nineteenth-century bibliography, in its infancy, so sadly needed. Bibliophily, however, like nature, abhors a vacuum. In consequence, all sorts of people rushed in where the angels did not deign to tread; and an area whose complexities had hardly begun to be realized, let alone surveyed, was invaded piecemeal by the enthusiastic amateurs of the author-bibliography. About fifty of these, of widely differing ambitions, appeared between the late seventies and the beginning of the first World War; and they mirror very accurately, especially in their duplications, the evolution—and the limitations—of contemporary taste in what were then "modern" authors. As for technique, they were compiled mainly to meet the requirements of collectors; and collectors do not normally ask for any more bibliography than they absolutely need.

Exceptions there were, like H. Buxton Forman's *A Shelley Library* (1876) and E. T. Cook's *Introduction to the Bibliography of Ruskin* (1912). But the pioneers were mostly satisfied with a very elementary descriptive formula, and from the turn of the century till the late twenties practice was dominated by the pattern set by Thomas J. Wise. This was, indeed, much ampler than anything hitherto attempted, and Wise paid full, if not always fully informed, attention to the details of original binding. Yet at bottom Wise was not so much a bibliographer as a collector and a dealer, who had the foresight and energy to develop a type of reference book which would supply the special needs of both fraternities. This was, and must always be, something different from the dispassionate, detached elucidation of an author's printed output, for which the bibliographer's public, though it will doubtless include collectors, includes many other kinds of user also.

The attack on a neglected period or field of bibliography can seldom, in an unregulated world, be planned. The nineteenth century, for the first fifty years after it began to be tackled at all, was the object of a series of isolated incursions by author-bibliographers; more or less technically skilful, more or less accurate, more or less scholarly in annotation, but in no case operating from adequately prepared positions. Their observation of the background had to be empirical, for there was no map. Their methods were unsystematic, for there was no system. They knew little and cared not much more about the history of book-structure and publishing practice during a century in which these factors were of paramount importance for the understanding of the books they were describing; for those who might have laid the foundations of research and erected a structure of theory had been otherwise occupied.

Publishing history, on which we lay so much emphasis today, is a wide term.

It includes [if I may quote Mr. Sadleir again] every incident, mishap or change of policy which may occur in the life of any book from the moment when a contract is made for its publication to the moment (maybe many years later) when it goes finally and irrevocably off the market, even the last copy of a remainder issue having been sold. The bibliographer may, therefore, be called upon to show knowledge or understanding of the relationship between author and publisher; the type of contract usual at any period (against which background exceptional arrangements shine like good deeds or glower like evil ones); the fashion for part-issue merging into that for magazine serial; the processes of book manufacture—paper, typography, illustration, binding and end-papers—in vogue at different times; the machinery of sale by publisher to wholesaler, retailer and circulating library, involving trade terms and other technicalities; the sequence of 'secondary' [bindings] and of cheaper editions and their physical qualities; the publisher-jobber who sold other firms' sheets over his own imprint; the gradual development of the remainder as we understand it today.

This, as the maestro admits, is a tall order. Yet bibliographers of eighteenth-century authors have given us exemplary models: Professor Pottle for Boswell, Miss Norton for Gibbon, Mr. Hazen for Strawberry Hill, to name no more. Mr. Sadleir himself, in his Trollope, set a standard for nineteenth-century author-bibliography which has not yet been improved upon. Even more pertinent, perhaps, was his Bibliographia Series of studies in book-structure and publishing practice: studies which, before they were discontinued, had begun to lay a few of the foundation-stones for that comprehensive treatise on nineteenth-century bibliography which is so badly needed.

I have generalized enough, perhaps more than enough, and those of you who have had to wrestle—at least for me it is wrestling—with half-sheet imposition, corrections at press, the evidential importance of binder's waste in localizing a binding, the function of longitudinal labels, the significance of press figures, or any of the hundred and one other problems in the bibliography of earlier books; you may well be asking whether the alleged complexities in nineteenth-century book-structure are really as complex as I have been leading you to suppose. Let me, then, offer some examples of what I mean. These are all features characteristic of, even if not peculiar to, nineteenth-century books. Mention of them may be found in most bibliographies of authors of the period. Yet for none of them is there any uniformity of treatment in bibliographical description; for none of them can the student assume any basis of agreement among the specialists; for none of them can he refer to any generally recognized authority.

This term is common enough in bibliographies of early nineteenth-century books, in the catalogues of antiquarian booksellers and auctioneers, and in the mouths of collectors and librarians. Although it will not be found (nor *boards* alone either) in the index to McKerrow,[1] Bowers [2] or Esdaile,[3] those of us who have occasion to use it presumably think we know what it means, and suppose that others will understand that meaning when we apply the term to a particular copy of a particular book. But do we? In the strictly limited sense of a boarded covering to the book not preceded by any other covering, yes; but that is not ten per cent of the weight of meaning which the term *original boards* is commonly made to bear. The physical differences between various styles of boarding (sometimes significant but seldom differentiated) are of small importance by comparison with the functional assumption which almost universally underlies the adjective *original*; the assumption that original boards are the publishers' binding. We know that paper-backed boards, with or without printed paper title-labels, had been widely adopted, well before 1800, as an intentionally temporary covering for books as distributed through the trade. We also know that some copies were subsequently sold in this form across the counter to those purchasers who still preferred employing their own binder to buying their books in a bookseller's leather binding. And there can be little doubt that by the turn of the century most publishers were putting up part of the edition of most books in boards. In as far, therefore, as a publisher's uniform can be postulated at all for English books of the first quarter of the nineteenth century (excluding books

[1] *Op. cit.* [2] *Op. cit.* [3] *A Student's Manual of Bibliography*, 1931.

slender enough to be served by wrappers), it was more likely to have been boards than anything else.

But can we assume that any given copy, however indubitably clothed in *original* boards, is therefore of necessity in the *publisher's* original boards? We cannot; for we have at present no means of distinguishing between publisher's boards, wholesaler's boards, and retailer's boards. So long as any substantial part of the edition of a newly published book continued to be supplied by the publisher to the trade in unbound quires—and this practice survived the general adoption of edition-binding in cloth—no copy in boards can be ascribed to the publisher with any confidence simply on the strength of the fact that the boards are "original."

Let me give an example. We happen to have access [1] to the subscription lists of two novels published in 1834—that is, in the second decade of publisher's cloth—by the London firm of Bentley: Maria Edgeworth's *Helen*, published on 22 February, and Bulwer Lytton's *The Last Days of Pompeii*, published on 29 September. The list price of each book was 31/6 in boards, the regular trade price in quires 22/6, and the special price on subscription day for copies in quires 21/3, with a bonus of 25 copies as 24. The total subscription for *Helen* was 793 as 769, for *Pompeii* 729 as 706. In both cases every single copy was taken in quires, for boarding or binding to their own order by wholesalers, booksellers and circulating libraries. Prominent on the subscription list were such publishers and exporters as Longman, Hamilton, Richardson, Smith Elder, Saunders and Otley; with Hookham, Hatchard, Cawthorne and others representing the libraries. Yet even the ordinary retail booksellers who took only three or four copies reckoned to provide their own binding.

Consequently, on publication day not one copy of either

[1] From the Private Catalogue of the firm of Bentley.

book in the publisher's binding passed across a bookshop or library counter; and (aside from review and complimentary copies) Bentley-bound copies would have been issued only to supply post-publication orders for copies not in quires.

Although a second edition of *The Last Days of Pompeii*, in two volumes, was published on 30 March 1835, copies of the first edition survive in at least seven different styles of "original" binding—(*a*) blue-grey boards with white paper backs, (*b*) drab boards with white paper backs, (*c*) all-over drab boards, (*d*) half cloth (i.e. paper board sides, cloth spine), (*e*) steel-blue morocco-grain cloth, (*f*) smooth plum-coloured cloth—all these with paper title-labels—and (*g*) maroon fine-ribbed cloth, gilt-lettered. The example in steel-blue cloth (*e*) was the publisher's file copy and presumably therefore in "publisher's binding." But the only copy I have seen in the plum cloth (style (*f*) and one of the copies I have seen in paper-backed boards (style *a*) contained an inserted catalogue of Longmans & Co., the wholesalers, who had taken up 200 copies of the 729 subscribed; and the catalogue in the boarded copy was dated September 1834, the month of publication. Will anyone dare to say what was "*the* original publisher's binding" for *The Last Days of Pompeii*? I think not.

Novels, we know, were handled through a somewhat specialized system of wholesale distribution until about mid-century. These two books may have been exceptional, even among novels. Yet the evidence I have summarized throws a salutary light on the still widely held misconception that *original boards* on a nineteenth-century book not only may be, but must be, the publisher's binding.

BOOKS ISSUED IN PARTS

Publication in parts dates from the eighteenth century and it continues today. But its heyday was the nineteenth century, when not only reference books and expensive picture books and cheap popular reissues for the bookstall trade, but also much fiction, many illustrated editions and a far larger number of general publications than is generally realized, were first issued to the public in this particular kind of instalment. The familiar part-issues, to most of us, are those of the popular Victorian novelists—Dickens, Thackeray, Trollope, Lever, Surtees and the rest—whose publishers exploited the method so successfully between 1837 and the early seventies; and if I restrict myself to these in the present context it is not because the part-issues of Dalziel's *Arabian Nights* (1863/4) or Herbert Spencer's *First Principles* (1862) are not equally apposite. But the best-selling novels are not only better documented: they also pose more obviously and more sharply the sort of questions about part-issue publication in general which do not seem to me to have been satisfactorily answered in the past.

I know of no treatise—or even any extended discussion —on the part-issue as a method of publishing.[1] The part-issues of individual nineteenth-century authors have, indeed, been dealt with by author-bibliographers and cataloguers of collections; and while these findings have been accepted by students with varying degrees of docility, only two such bibliographies have treated part-issues really seriously;[2] Sadleir's *Trollope* and Hatton and Cleaver's *Dickens*. (Van Duzer's *Thackeray* is a primitive work by today's standards, as Mr. David Randall's researches into *Vanity Fair* have recently reminded us; almost equally so is Locke's *Ainsworth*; Lever, who published many of his novels in parts, still awaits his bibliographer; and the

[1] But see N. G. Wiles, *Serial Fiction*, Cambridge University Press, 1956.
[2] The occasional part-issues of Captain Marryat, J. S. Le Fanu and other authors included in Mr. Sadleir's *XIX Century Fiction* (1951) are authoritatively treated.

Surtees entries in Schwerdt's *Hunting, Hawking and Shooting* are both unreliable and ill-founded.)

Michael Sadleir's *Trollope, a Bibliography* tells us not only nearly everything about Trollope's part-issues, but also more about Victorian fiction-publishing in this form than can be found anywhere else that I know of. Even though these valuable generalizations are scattered up and down the book, Mr. Sadleir understood the economics, the production methods, and the distribution arrangements of part-issue publication; and this knowledge saved his readers from certain misconceptions which have been foisted on to the bibliography of Dickens by Messrs. Hatton and Cleaver. Their book [1] provided a more elaborate description of their author's numerous part-issues than had ever been attempted before, or is ever likely to be attempted again; and they brought a massive sort of order into the description of text, plates and wrappers. This was of general as well as particular value in that they showed how often the text of one part or another was reprinted, and how often worn plates were replaced, before the completion of the series. They proved that for several books duplicate sets of steel plates (not absolutely identical) were etched before printing even started. They laid, in short, a number of ghosts which had haunted Dickens bibliography for decades. They did not, however, appreciate how tenuous, how uncontrolled, how liable to accident or caprice, was the connection between the text and plates of a part-issued book with that mass of advertising matter generally wrappered with it. They not only treated this as if it were bibliographically almost as important as the text—a delusion common to most part-issue collectors of the older school. They laid down a canon for its composition. In this they bowed lowest before the rarest inserted slips which (apart from the possibilities inherent in careless or

[1] *A Bibliography of the Periodical Works of Charles Dickens*, 1933.

170

malicious "making-up") are *ipso facto* the least likely to
have been units in any planned composition of advertising
matter. And they ignored entirely the probability that
most of the advertising contracts for a best-selling part-
issue were handled by an agent, so that even the publisher
saw the results only when the first copies of each part were
delivered on his table.

We may smile indulgently today at the passion of the
part-issue collector for "the very rare cork slip in Part II."
But there are other bibliographical problems connected
with part-issues which are no laughing matter. The most
taxing of them lie in the debatable relationship, especially
in respect of priority, between the series of wrapped parts
and the several alternative forms in which the complete
work may be found.

(*a*) It was a common, though not universal, practice for
the publisher to issue the book in volume form just before
distribution of the final number of the part-issue. Which is
the first published edition?

(*b*) If, as often, there had been reprinting of individual
parts or alterations in plates during the course of part-issue,
which might be spread over more than a year, the quires
gathered for binding in volume form would presumably be
of the latest *state*. Yet they might be of the earliest *issue*.

(*c*) A part-issued novel in its volume form would often
be available from the publisher, as countless advertisements
show, in alternative bindings of cloth, half-leather, and full
leather; and these need cause us no more trouble than
any other simultaneous binding variants. But it was also
common practice for the publisher to advertise his readiness,
at stated charges, to put serially issued sets of parts into one
or other of such bindings for any faithful subscriber who
liked to send them in, after completion of the series. If the
result can be identified (as it sometimes can, by the stab-
holes surviving from the wrapped parts), what is its

relationship to an edition-bound copy in the same style of binding? Its interior is earlier, but its covering is later.

(*d*) Furthermore, it was often open to purchasers of a set of parts to apply to the publisher for a cloth case in which his local binder could enclose them. The local binder would usually trim and sometimes gild or sprinkle the edges. The result is not edition-binding: but it is nevertheless publisher's binding. How will the stickler for priority *and* original condition rate such a copy *vis-à-vis* an edition-bound copy, which has uncut edges and was bound first, but whose text and plates will usually be of the latest throughout?

You may well think this hair-splitting as wearisome as the fuss made elsewhere about the presence or absence from a set of parts of a pink slip advertising hair lotion. I have, indeed, deliberately carried it a little further than would be thought strictly necessary by a reasonable bibliographer. My point is that none of us can decide what is reasonable and what is not until all the facts have been examined, and the questions they provoke not only asked but answered.

CANCELS

We are all aware that the device for correction, suppression, or addition applied to a book already completely printed off, which is known as cancelling, includes anything from a pasted-on slip carrying a single word to the reprinting of several leaves for substitution. Yet the fact that single-leaf cancels outnumber all others by about fifty to one in books printed before the second quarter of the nineteenth century has helped, if only subconsciously, to inhibit full consideration of the type of text-cancel which grew progressively commoner with the increased mechanization of printing. As time and labour became more important, paper and type-metal cheaper, printers and publishers found it to be generally simpler and less expensive to mend a page by reprinting, not the single leaf, which would have to be pasted on to the prepared stub of its conjugate, but the quarter-sheet, the half-sheet, or even the whole sheet. I cannot find that the bibliographers have laid down the maximum number of substitute leaves, reprinted in one operation for insertion in one place, which still qualify for the term *cancel*. Certainly, none of them seems to have faced the fact that a substitute gathering does not differ in essentials, though it will in its method of insertion, from a single substitute leaf. And if it is hard to tell, of a single-leaf cancel, whether it was effected before publication (making a *state*) or after (making an *issue*), it is twice as hard to tell of a multi-leaved cancel.

Except for a couple of references to cancelled title-leaves, which have remained and doubtless will remain common, Dr. R. W. Chapman's monograph on *Cancels* [1] deals with no example later than 1825. This was perhaps natural in an eighteenth-century man; and his was, certainly, a cancel-ridden century; yet I find that other authorities have paid hardly more attention to the development of this practice in more recent times. Author-bibliographers have normally recorded, and sometimes analysed, cancels in individual books; but these again have usually been those single-leaf cancels which are so much easier to detect, and of which examples have persisted despite the prevailing modern practice.

The presence of a single-leaf cancel may be betrayed by the stub, by a signature on what would normally be an unsigned leaf, by the paper, by any one of half a dozen signals familiar to the student of earlier books. Have we any such guidance for the post-mechanization types of cancel? Do we know whether printers in 1830 or 1880 slit the *cancellandum* at the foot as a signal to the binder? Is there any substitute, in books printed on wove paper, for

[1] Bibliographia Series, No. 3, 1930.

the evidence of cancellation provided in laid paper by the watermark or the chain-lines? Did the Victorian printer always—or ever—sign the *cancellans*; and if the *cancellantia* were plural—up to, say, four leaves—would he have signed only the first? Did printers consider a reprinted gathering, and did binders treat it, as the equivalent of a cancel in the eighteenth-century sense? If so, ought bibliographers to follow them? If so, again, how (when identified) are multi-leaved cancels to be described in the more abbreviated formulae for collation?

I do not pretend to know the answers to any of these questions, or to a dozen more on the same subject for which I have no breath left at the moment. But I cannot help feeling that they need attention.

BINDING VARIANTS

I have already said a word or two about boards as an original binding. This style, and its hybrid, half-cloth with paper labels, persisted until mid-century for fiction, and longer for verse and other slender or self-conscious volumes. But edition-binding in cloth, at the expense of the publisher, had become general within fifteen or twenty years of its adoption by William Pickering in the early 1820's. It was in 1832 that Archibald Leighton solved the second of the two main technical problems: the manufacture of a "filler" for the fabric which would take the dye smoothly, and the process for stamping gilt lettering and decoration direct on to the cloth. By 1840, then, publisher's cloth was not only the normal covering for finished copies of most books, with the exception of three-decker fiction. It was a uniform: so that the bibliographer, the librarian and the book-collector might be expected to be able to say with confidence, of an individual copy, "this is (or is not) in its original, publisher's binding."

Would that it were so simple! I do not propose to insult

your intelligence by explaining that publishers very often bind from printed stock in batches, or by expatiating on the sort of variations which this habit produces. I am going to assume that most of you are familiar with Michael Sadleir's pioneer work, *The Evolution of Publishers' Binding Styles*,[1] and that some of you may have looked into certain subsidiary studies by another hand.[2] I commend to you, in the same context, Mr. Sadleir's bibliographical catalogue, *XIX Century Fiction*,[3] in which he has expanded and refined our system of nomenclature for cloth fabrics,[4] besides making a further attack on the intractable problem of the accurate description of colours. He has also distinguished one or two fresh categories of binding variant; and it is these which I want to pursue here.

For the classification of binding variants in English nineteenth-century books is still at a provisional stage. Such as it is, it has been worked out, during the twenty years or so since anyone began to pay attention to such things, by two people only. Neither of them would claim to be an analytical bibliographer, even though Mr. Sadleir has been President of the Bibliographical Society; and one of them at least would like to shed some of the responsibility for stabilizing the system on a sound and agreed basis. Otherwise a temporary structure may become rigid simply from

[1] Bibliographia Series, No. 1, 1930.

[2] *Binding Variants in English Publishing, 1820–1900*, Bibliographia Series, No. 6, 1932; *More Binding Variants*, 1938; *Publisher's Cloth, an Outline History*, 1935. All three by the present writer.

[3] London, Constable; California University Press, Los Angeles, 1951.

[4] What must, I suppose, be called the Sadleir-Carter system, developed over the past 25 years, is a combination of traditional and descriptive terminology. It lends itself readily to the study of the history of cloth fabric for binding, and for nineteenth-century English books I for one still consider it to be the most generally serviceable. But the Bibliographical Society of America has now set its imprimatur (in Mr. Jacob Blanck's *Bibliography of American Literature*, Vol. I, New Haven, 1955) on the code lettering system, keyed (up to a point) to the manufacturers' specimen books. My reasons for discarding this system in 1930 are set out on pp. xvi–xviii of *Binding Variants in English Publishing, 1820–1900*, published under Mr. Sadleir's aegis two years later.

being constantly used by people who have not been offered either constructive criticism or any alternative.

Let us leave on one side such special styles as trial bindings, advance-issue bindings, author's bindings, gift bindings and library bindings. Let us also avert our eyes from the difficult period—roughly from the early thirties to the late fifties—when many novels were issued concurrently in half cloth, paper labels, and full cloth, gilt-lettered. Let us ignore simultaneous colour-variants, and books published alternatively in cloth and in printed wrappers. Let us simply consider the elementary sequence *primary*, *secondary* and *remainder*.

Where variant bindings have been observed on different copies of the same edition, the term *primary* has been used for that one which can be shown to be the earliest (exclusive of trial or advance copies): i.e., the one in which copies were distributed on publication day. A *remainder* binding is one which can be shown to have been put on, whether or not by the original publisher, for another publisher or wholesaler who had bought the fag-end of the edition in sheets or quires for binding and distribution on his own account, usually at a reduced price. These two are the top and the bottom of the priority scale; and although it is not always easy to identify the primary binding for a particular book, there cannot be much argument about the denotation.

But between these two there may be a distracting number of variants, often minor but sometimes considerable. There are, for instance, at least nine distinct binding variants of Browning's *Sordello* (1840) and the same number of Meredith's *The Shaving of Shagpat* (1856). Can we wonder at the variants [1] for the Brontë sisters' *Poems*, published in 1846 by Aylott and Jones, and taken over (after at least two bindings-up) by Smith Elder, when we

[1] See M. L. Parrish, *Victorian Lady Novelists*, 1933.

look at the entries in the latter's ledger?[1]   They run thus:

November 1848	Stock purchased from Aylott & Jones	961 copies
July 1, 1853	Stock in hand—quires 656⎫ cloth 26⎭	682 copies
June 1, 1854	Stock in hand—quires 630⎫ cloth 20⎭	650 copies

Binding orders given: 1853   25 copies @ 38/—per 100
                          1854   51 copies   —
                          1855   50 copies   —
                          1857 [2] 450 copies @ 34/—per 100

Even eleven years, and at least six bindings, after publication, there were still over a hundred copies in quires in the publisher's warehouse.

There is nothing abnormal about such a record for a nineteenth-century book. The question is, whether the single term *secondary* is an adequate umbrella to cover all successive variants between an undoubted primary and a possible remainder, or whether we need some subdivision. Twenty years' use of it in its original, deliberately simple, connotation would, I think, have convinced me that nicer distinctions are needed, even if I had not been from time to time distressed to see the uses to which the unassuming A's, B's and C's of my book on *Binding Variants* were being put by those who suffer from, or cater to, that morbid yearning for priority which I have elsewhere [3] diagnosed as "the chronological obsession." For at present the single term *secondary* not only has to serve for any one of the possibly numerous binding variants which followed the primary, but also—and more important—it is applied impartially to those which represent an intentional change of style, made on the publisher's order, and to those which circumstances or accident imposed on the binder.

[1] By courtesy of John Murray.
[2] The year Mrs. Gaskell's *Life of Charlotte Brontë* came out.
[3] *ABC for Book-Collectors*.

It is not always easy, a hundred years later, to tell whether a variant before us which looks like a secondary owes its variations to the publisher's saying "let's use a cheaper cloth and cut out some of the decoration," or to the binder, when the order comes through for "100 as before, by Friday week," being temporarily unable to match the original fabric and having mislaid the brass die for the ornament on the spine. Yet the difference between these two classes of secondary is a real one, even if it must often remain theoretical.

Professor Bowers, who is reluctant to admit that the publisher's binding is an integral part of the book, naturally takes a dim view of binding variants in general. Pardonably affronted by the excessive claims made for some of them, he denies any of them the right to qualify as an *issue*: reserving this classification to the sheets of the book and roundly declaring that "variations resulting from binding-up lots of sheets constitute states of the binding and nothing else."[1] Mr. Sadleir is not so brusque as this. He too has felt the need for discipline among the more fanatical variant-hunters; but to an all-round down-grading he has preferred a suggested distinction between the significant variants and the insignificant. I am not happy about his use of the term *substitute* for a secondary binding to which the publisher is known to have switched owing to some dissatisfaction with the primary (e.g., the removal of the bows of ribbon from Marie Corelli's *Wormwood*, 1890, because the circulating libraries objected); for I am reluctant to introduce for such a rare category an additional term which makes a distinction between one kind of intentional variation and another, until we have dealt with the more important distinction between the intentional and the unintentional. For this Mr. Sadleir has at least partially provided by the use of the term *second binding* to denote a

[1] *Op. cit.*, p. 414.

demonstrably later binding, differing slightly if at all from
the primary, which may be reasonably acquitted of resulting from any order for a change given by the publisher.
Such a term is certainly needed, and this one seems on the
face of it apt enough. Yet it does not fit very comfortably
into the originally arbitrary but now widely accepted
sequence of *primary* and *secondary*.

One of the most realistic of modern American philosophers has laid it down that "a book is a book is a book".
Professor Bowers adds "whether it has a cover or not."
It is tempting to acquiesce in this wholesale dismissal
of binding variants from our bibliographical agenda, and
I am not suggesting that the line of least resistance is
necessarily the wrong one to take. If, however, we reject
the Bowers *Diktat* in favour of that increased articulation of
terminology towards which Mr. Sadleir seems to be moving, it is not too late, but it is certainly not too soon, for a
radical review of the whole subject. It is, after all, twenty
years since the first and last we have had.

INSERTED ADVERTISEMENTS

Inserted publishers' catalogues were not unknown in the
eighteenth century, and they were still common during the
first decade or two of the twentieth. But they were a
regular feature of nineteenth-century book-making; they
are more often bibliographically useful in nineteenth-
century books than in others; and more nonsense has been
talked about them by collectors and booksellers than about
almost any other item in the bibliophile's vocabulary. We
have already glanced at one particularly harassing class of
advertising matter: that customarily inserted in wrappered
serial parts. But although, like part-issues, yellow-backs
and other cheap books sometimes carried unbookish
advertising, the usual insertion, if any, was of one or more
sheets of a publisher's, a wholesaler's—occasionally, in

early days, a bookseller's—list of books for sale. By far the commonest form of this in the nineteenth century was a publisher's catalogue of his new publications, printed in bulk and furnished to his binder for inclusion in all, or certain specified, titles on his list as they came forward for binding. Such catalogues were usually dated; and it is the evidence from these dates which has been so strained and misused by the issue-mongers and point-maniacs as to induce, in the bibliographical purists, a disinclination to have anything to do with inserted advertisements at all.

I often share their indignation. I am no party to the theory that, because fifty copies of a certain book have been noted with a publisher's catalogue, a fifty-first need ever have had one or needs one now. I cherish the proved cases of copies of an edition with (say) October advertisements having been issued later than those with advertisements dated December. I have watched catalogues being inserted in modern binderies, and seen what happens when the pile runs out. I am, I hope, as profoundly sceptical of bibliographical hypotheses which depend on evidence from inserted advertisements as anyone in England (or for that matter in the state of Illinois, which as you know is rather larger in area). But no one who is working seriously at nineteenth-century bibliography can afford to look down his nose at any evidence, however suspiciously it needs to be handled, however well it deserves Professor Bowers's disdainful epithet, "collateral."

There can be no doubt that a copy of Trollope's *The Warden* with a catalogue dated 1858 must be of a late binding-up, for the book was published in 1855. Mr. Sadleir calls this a *second binding*, Dr. Bowers would call it a later "state" of the binding; but neither of them disputes the evidence of the catalogue. This is a simple example. A hundred like it could be cited without difficulty. But there are thousands of others where the time-difference between two catalogues, found impartially in otherwise identical copies of the same edition, is only a matter of a month or two; and though the details of these must be recorded, unsupported inferences from them will be cheerfully excused. Much less common, but much more interesting, are inserted advertisements which throw light on, or raise questions about, not priority of issue, but some aspect of the publishing history of the book. For example, end-papers printed with Chapman and Hall advertisements of the late seventies have been noted, in association with secondary bindings, in copies of books whose title-pages bear dates between 1844 and 1873 and the imprints of Blackwood, Bradbury and Evans, Bentley, Sampson Low, Tinsley, Strahan, and Charles Knight.[1] Some day we may find out why. Of Dickens's *Edwin Drood*, published in 1870, DNB and his bibliographer record that 50,000 copies were sold: a record even for Dickens. Yet the second, and commonest, of the three binding styles so far noted on copies in volume form almost always contains a W. H. Smith list of "remainders," dated 1872. Can we doubt that *Edwin Drood* itself was remaindered? And could we have guessed it without this evidence? Earlier in the century remainder publishers and jobbers, like Tegg, Templeman and A. K. Newman, would often have their own catalogues bound up with a consignment bought from the original publisher in quires; and if the binding was of half cloth or boards, these catalogues may be the only evidence of the book's transfer.

During the boards-and-label period, indeed, that preference for individual binding arrangements which I have already emphasized was constantly exemplified in inserted catalogues alien to the imprint on the title-page of the book. A dozen or so are recorded by Mr. Sadleir in his catalogue,

[1] See *More Binding Variants*, p. 51; Sadleir, *XIX Century Fiction*, No 353.

and I could double the list from my own notebooks. But until the bibliographers come to some decision about the status of a first edition published by X but demonstrably boarded for Y, and until (perhaps a couple of decades thereafter?) that decision is generally accepted by book-collectors, so long will the bookseller remain under the temptation to save his prospective customer from a bibliographical headache by a not usually too difficult piece of excision. And while I agree that inserted advertisements cause an amount of trouble and uncertainty disproportionate to the quantity of conclusive evidence which we have so far learned to extract from them, yet they have their implications and they must surely not be neglected.

DUST-JACKETS

My last excursion is going to be a very short one. The dust-jacket will remain an intractable problem to bibliographers until they can all agree, first whether it is or is not to be considered part of the volume at all, and secondly how to be sure, without a cast-iron pedigree, whether the jacket on an individual copy really belongs to it. When these elementary questions have been answered, there will remain the problem of the proper formula for describing such of the dust-jacket's contents as are deemed worth recording. These are difficulties which many students of nineteenth-century bibliography comfortably suppose to be outside their period. If there are any such wishful thinkers among my audience, let me remind them that one dust-jacket survives [1] (and not a primitive-looking one either), printed for (and when first seen by me, still wrapped round) a book published in the year 1832. Consequently, for every year of dust-jacket trouble which

---

[1] Alas, it survives no longer, except in photographic reproduction: having been lost somewhere between All Souls College and the Bodleian five years ago.

besets the twentieth-century bibliographer, you nineteenth-century men have a year and a half.

These are but a few symptoms of the present confused state of nineteenth-century bibliography as it appears to one groping observer. We are concerned just now only with English books, but an equally depressing list of problems peculiar to American books would be easy enough to compile. It is not that anything happened between 1800 and 1900 to invalidate the general principles enunciated by McKerrow. It is rather that the standardization of book-production, the technological developments in printing and binding, the changes in distribution methods and in reading habits, are factors that combine to impose on a system of bibliography adequate for hand-printed books a weight of subdivision and expansion which most practitioners have found intolerable. The result has been that the amateurs have gradually built a sort of hand-me-down superstructure on bibliographical foundations which remain essentially enumerative, while the experts who could have laid sound foundations have, with a few exceptions, held aloof from a difficult, unrewarding and perhaps in their eyes rather undignified task.

McKerrow, who was no recluse but an active director of a firm of London publishers, talked excellent sense about modern books; but unfortunately not enough of it. We should be thankful that the most energetic and wide-ranging of contemporary bibliographical theorists, even if his heart is in the seventeenth century, has recognized the plight of the modern book and has not ignored his duty to it. I refer to Professor Fredson Bowers, of the University of Virginia, who devoted a hundred pages of his *Principles of Bibliographical Description* to the nineteenth and twentieth centuries. These pages are no easier reading than the rest of the book; some of us may dissent from some of Professor Bowers's judgments; others will feel that he seems more acutely conscious of twentieth-century problems than nineteenth. Yet he is the only bibliographical pundit who has not only seen the need for an appendix to McKerrow but has made a serious attempt to provide it. And if I differ from him, on points of detail, in my estimate of the best way of tackling the task still before us, it must be understood that I do so with diffidence and with great respect.

Professor Bowers concurs in Michael Sadleir's view of the reasons why the theory and principles of nineteenth-century bibliography have been neglected. Of the result he roundly states that "there is scarcely a nineteenth-century author of literary importance whose bibliography is not either outdated or fundamentally unsound." One may murmur questioningly—Scott, Jane Austen, Hazlitt, Trollope, Meredith, Samuel Butler, Oscar Wilde? But one must admit Byron, Tennyson, Dickens, Thackeray, and many more; and there will be little dissent from Professor Bowers's prime *desideratum*—"an authoritative manual for study which will do for nineteenth- and twentieth-century books what McKerrow's *Introduction to Bibliography* did for hand-printed publications." His own ample and detailed treatment of bibliographical principles and practice for the study of modern books is likely to be regarded as the interim authority; and it is because we may have to wait some time for our new McKerrow that it is our duty to examine the Bowers findings with the closest attention. For here is a powerful—indeed an autocratic—intelligence, addicted to formula and impatient of imprecision, at large in an area whose bibliography is still in a highly fluid, and therefore vulnerable, state.

Professor Bowers's thesis is that "if bibliography of machine-printed books is to take its place in scholarship beside the best work devoted to older books, it must be conceived and executed for scholarly purposes." This is unexceptionable; but he sometimes reacts from "the excesses of undiscriminating commercialism" to a position in which it almost seems that collectors and their interests are outside the pale of scholarship. Scholarship, in this context, surely does not end with the mere text: it embraces book-structure, publishing practice, copyright regulations and the remuneration of authorship, distribution methods and reading habits. And these can sometimes be illuminated by bibliographical evidence of a kind which gets short shrift from Professor Bowers.[1] Admittedly there has been too much insistence on "points," too frequent a treatment as abnormalities of what are really structural commonplaces. But the pendulum can swing too far the other way.

Professor Bowers has proposed some valuable simplifications. For instance, his suggestion for redefining *issue* and *state* in terms of purpose rather than of chronology seems to me to call for the most sympathetic study. In general, however, I should have welcomed a firmer application, over the whole field, of that principle of degressive bibliography to which I referred earlier. Madan's conception of the descriptive formula suitable to a modern book is admittedly altogether out of date, and Madan would have been the first to say so today. But as one studies the Bowers formula —and a single formula for 150 years ignores the degressive principle—it is permissible to wonder not so much whether it asks too much of potential bibliographers, as whether it is not unnecessarily elaborate for many of the books for which it is designed. Professor Bowers has thought much harder about our period than most of his predecessors. But his attack on the nineteenth century has been conducted from a seventeenth-century base, and the tactics

---

[1] But see Professor Bowers's subsequent paper, "Purposes of Descriptive Bibliography, with Some Remarks on Method," in the *Library*, Fifth Series, Vol. VIII, No. 1, March 1953.

occasionally show signs of the rigidity natural to a cautious man operating in comparatively unfamiliar territory.

The trouble is that a confident elasticity of bibliographical treatment, which seems to me essential for modern books, presupposes thorough familiarity with a comprehensive body of background study. This, for the nineteenth century, is not yet available. And it is in this direction, I suggest, that our most urgent agenda are to be found. We may continue to demand, and ourselves to observe, a more thoughtful approach to author-bibliography. But this is not enough; for practice needs to be firmly based on a foundation of accepted principle. I do not believe "the modern McKerrow" can be written until that commanding theorist, its author, has at his disposal a whole series of technical treatises on those many aspects of book-production and distribution in which the nineteenth century differs so radically from its predecessors. The guerilla incursions of the average author-bibliographer have in the past proved ineffective and sometimes misleading. Collectors and specialists have made valuable contributions, but they have been isolated efforts. Mr. Sadleir and his Bibliographia Series indicated the pattern, but pioneers must be followed up in force. Professor Bowers's magisterial treatise is at once a landmark and a challenge.

PART SIX

Two Frivolities

OPERATION SHUCKBURGH[1]

BACKGROUND appreciation: Intelligence reports received
late in December 1950 indicated the possible presence of a
hitherto unlocated copy of the *Gutenberg Bible* in a private
library "somewhere in England." M.I.47 (Muniments and
Black Letter Section) were naturally sceptical, since such
reports (usually second or third hand) are commonly found
on investigation to refer to any Bible printed in gothic
type and/or in a foreign language and more than a hundred
years old, but otherwise of no interest and often lacking
the title-page.

---

[1] This piece was first published in the *Bookseller*, 17 February 1951.
It describes, with a perhaps unseemly levity, the purchase and transport
across the Atlantic of a copy of the 42-line Bible, commonly known as the
Gutenberg Bible, which had disappeared from bibliographical ken for
more than a century and a quarter. Bought in the eighteenth century by
Sir George Shuckburgh, Bt., this copy of the greatest of all printed books
had been mentioned, in the past tense, by Dibdin in 1824. It had subsequently descended, through a series of female lines and by bequests no
more obvious to Debrett than to De Ricci (who listed it as *"exemplaire
disparue"* in his census of 1911), to Lady Christian Martin. Her possession
of it came to the knowledge of Messrs Quaritch and myself from a source
which I naturally neither had nor have the slightest intention of com-
promising. We negotiated jointly for its purchase on behalf of an
American collector who had recently enjoined Scribners of New York
(whose European representative I then was) to procure her a copy. Being
offered the Shuckburgh copy within three months of this injunction—a
promptitude of response against which professionals at least would probably have laid odds of more than a hundred to one—she declined it (not on
grounds of the price). Messrs Quaritch being at this point ready to dis-
pose of their interest in the book, the late Mr. Charles Scribner, with a
confidence in his Rare Book Department which I shall always gratefully
admire, bought the Shuckburgh Gutenberg for stock. It is now in the
private collection of Mr. Arthur A. Houghton of New York (for details
see Mr. Edward Lazare's latest census in the *Antiquarian Bookman 1956
Yearbook*).

187

In this case, however, Dring and Howard (Quaritch's Horse), two very reliable officers, decided after thorough sifting of the available evidence that the objective itself had been accurately identified. At this stage it was impossible to be sure whether it was at full strength or had been adequately maintained during the 125 years since it had last been listed in a responsible battle-order (Dibdin, Thomas Frognall, *Library Companion*, 1824, vol. II, p. 13, footnote).

Further reconnaissance was ordered; and this was succeeded by a period of brief but intense patrol activity. It was essential that these operations be conducted with the fullest regard for secrecy and for the security of our own line of communications. Moreover, every precaution was taken against infiltration by rival forces. In the event, the objective was successfully engaged; an armistice honourable to both sides was concluded; and a flying column under command of Dring was despatched to complete the first part of the operation.

Details of the succeeding phases are set out below, as summarized by your correspondent [1] from G.H.Q. logbook (by permission of Brigadier Palimpsest, M.B.E., Records Branch).

January 20th. 1200 hours: *Gutenberg Bible* arrives under escort at 11 Grafton Street. Found to be a magnificently large copy ($16\frac{1}{2} \times 11$ inches), substantially complete (lacking 5 of the 643 leaves), crisp and unmarked, first printing throughout, bound in crimson morocco by Walther (signed and dated 1789). Bookplate of Sir George Shuckburgh, Bt., in each volume. 1400 hours: Book taken to British Museum for collation and comparison with George III and Grenville copies. 1700 hours: Closing time. Howard and Carter (Scribner Foreign Legion) retire to winter

---

Who ought, no doubt, to admit his all too palpable indebtedness to *The New Yorker's* incomparable Mr. Stanley.

quarters. Fourth of a series of signals despatched to advance H.Q. (Scribners, New York).

January 22nd (Monday). 1030 hours: Examination resumed. 1315 hours: Examination concluded. Book put under guard in cells at 11 Grafton Street. 1800 hours: Fifth (extravagantly long) signal despatched to New York by cable.

January 23rd: Satisfactory return signal having been received from advance H.Q., New York, series of applications and requisitions delivered by despatch riders to Board of Trade, Bank of England, British Overseas Airways and other associated commands required to be put in the picture prior to securing of necessary movement orders.

January 25th. 0930 hours: Fast, lightly armoured detachment under command of Dust (seconded from Scribner base H.Q., London) retrieves movement orders, duly countersigned by appropriate authorities. 1145 hours: As part of prepared cover-plan, Carter shows self on sky-line in Pall Mall at private view of Lucius Wilmerding library, afterwards lunching in full view of fellow club-members with two librarians (one Oxford, one Cambridge). 1830–2200 hours: Howard and Carter (Dring having been ordered to hospital by M.O. with serious attack of euphoria) carry out next movement in cover-plan by adopting distant behaviour to each other at dinner of Antiquarian Booksellers' Association. Satisfactory lack of reaction observed.

January 26th. 1630 hours: Carter packs the two volumes (weight 36 lbs.) into somewhat disreputable suitcase. 1700 hours: B.O.A.C. officials at first decline to regard suitcase as "hand baggage" permissible to accompany passenger. Passenger declines board plane if suitcase detached from hand. Customer always right. 1800 hours: First aircraft ever to carry a *Gutenberg Bible* takes off from London Airport.

January 27th (Saturday). 0300–0400 hours: Coffee and tedium at Ceflavik Airport, Iceland (unscheduled but all too regular stop). 1130 hours, Eastern Seaboard time: Captain Jones touches down Boeing Stratocruiser like a feather at Idlewild Airport, New York. 1200–1300 hours: Task force encounters U.S. Customs, a heavily fortified area with minefields, road-blocks and defences in depth.

Commandant unable to make exception to rule that any commercial object valued at over $500 requires "pre-entry forms." Reinforcements arrive in shape of Scribners' customs broker, who outdoes himself in cajolery. Carter points out book non-dutiable on three grounds: (1) Bible, (2) printed in a foreign language, viz. Latin, (3) over twenty years old, viz. manufactured *c.* 1455. Opposition amiable, but implacable and well entrenched. Nothing doing till Monday morning. Task force compelled leave book in B.O.A.C. cargo shed, locked in a wire cage (too big for safe). Receipt reads: "One suitcase said to contain a Gutenberg Bible." 1330 hours: Double Bourbon, straight. 1340 hours: Ditto, with water. 1350 hours: Morale still poor, Carter leaves for New York City in large car (bullet-proof windows) provided by Scribners in anticipation of precious cargo, with one of the firm's vice-presidents intended as escort for same. 1530 hours: Report to Randall, O.C. advance H.Q., 597 Fifth Avenue. 1700 hours: Cover-plan continued: Randall and Carter ostentatiously unbusiness-like at Grolier Club tea party. Ugly moment when big middle-western collector sportively enquires what treasure Carter has brought with him—a *Gutenberg Bible*? Randall chokes in highball. Carter, who is, of course, in mufti, but has a smattering of the local dialect, fakes a light laugh and replies, "Only three copies of the *Bay Psalm Book* this time." Counter-attack apparently successful. Randall executes diversion to cover strategic withdrawal to unprepared positions.

January 29th (Monday). 1000 hours: Customs broker, armed with battery of double-barrelled, foolscap size, pre-entry forms (Mark IX), each loaded in quadruplicate, leaves downtown New York for Idlewild, with Carter in tow, in plain, unarmoured station wagon seconded for un-explained mission by Ronald Tree, Esq. 1050 hours: Task force engages defences. Progress slow but resistance weakening. 1140 hours: Appraiser approaches suitcase. 1141 hours: Carter insists on declaiming passage from letter written in 1870 by Henry Stevens, the London bookseller, to George Brinley, purchaser of the second *Gutenberg Bible* to cross the Atlantic, enjoining the raising of hats in the presence of the great book.[1] Customs officials some-what confused, being already hatless, but appear to be slightly shaken. 1145 hours: Suitcase opened and the book exposed. Customs officials now really impressed. 1150 hours: Book cleared through customs and escorted to New York. 1600 hours: Book inspected by Mr. Charles Scribner, for whose approval, and purchase if approved at a price already agreed, it has been brought to America. 1700 hours: Book stowed in Scribner safe, which, being normally used for authors' MSS, is considered quite secure even when not locked.

January 30th. 1030 hours: Staff conference. 1145 hours: Ceremonial parade at Pierpont Morgan Library. 1600 hours: Further staff conference.

January 31st: Mr. Scribner, after asking if there were not something rather cheaper he could buy for Randall and

---

[1] Full text: "Pray, Sir, ponder for a moment and appreciate the rarity and importance of this precious consignment from the old world to the new. Not only is it the first Bible, but it is the first book ever printed. It was read in Europe half a century before America was discovered. Please suggest to your deputy that he uncover his head while in the presence of this great book. Let no Custom House official, or other man in or out of authority, see it without first reverently raising his hat. It is not possible for many men ever to touch or even look upon a page of a Gutenberg Bible."

still make him happy, confirms purchase of the Bible.
Carter and Randall, now at last able to admit publicly that
this long-lost copy even so much as existed, emit studiously
modulated cries of pleasure. A signal is sent to Williams,
O.C. Base H.Q. (Quaritch, London). And the Shuckburgh copy of the *Gutenberg Bible*—unknown to census-
makers De Ricci (1911), Schwenke (1923), Reichner
(1927), Johnson (1932) or Lazare (1950)—takes its place
in the stock of the Scribner Rare Book Department (12
days, 3 hours, and 15 minutes after its arrival in London).

February 1st: All over bar the shouting.[1]

[1] And, of course, the small matter of finding a buyer for a fairly expensive book (the New York newspapers quoted us at the time as saying that
the purchaser "could not expect to get much change out of $200,000").

ABC FOR BOOK-COLLECTORS [1]

THE author of this book must be either a fool or a knave.
If he supposes that serious collectors are going to tolerate
any man's laying down the law and airing his views, to the
tune of about 450 alphabetical entries, on book-collecting,
bibliography, taste, technique, tactics, the auction room,
printing, binding, paper-making, illustration, publishing
history and a dozen other associated subjects, then he
clearly knows very little about bibliomania, which breeds
doctrinaires as opinionated and contentious as can be found
in any walk of life.

If, on the other hand, he has conceived the base notion
that beginners are humble enough to believe any claptrap
about the bibliophile mystery that they read in print, just
because an otherwise reputable publisher has been bam-
boozled into undertaking a book like this, then he is a
cynical ruffian: far more of a menace than the issue-
mongers, mint-condition fetishists, point-maniacs and
other strange fry whom he holds up to disapproval in the
course of his 190-odd pages.

Whichever explanation is the right one, the author of
this *ABC* is old enough to know better. He has been in
the rare-book business for a quarter of a century, affects a
familiarity with McKerrow, Proctor, STC and the rest,
and once held a readership (for a very brief period) at one
of the older universities.[2] His attempt to saddle an eminent
Treasury official[3] with the inspiration, and an equally

---

[1] This notice of my book *ABC for Book-Collectors* was published in
the *Bookseller*, 29 September 1952 (see Preface). It was signed: but the
authorship of the work under review was not given. A few footnotes are
now added.

[2] The Sanders Readership in Bibliography in the University of Cambridge (an annual appointment).

[3] E. W. Playfair, C.B.

eminent man of letters [1] with the "fostering," of such a project as this, merely adds insult to injury.

It is true that the author's earlier books have been praised in some quarters, and are even cited here and there in catalogues and works of reference, so that the uninstructed might suppose him entitled to the benefit of the doubt when he produces another. But it must not be forgotten that for several of these he somehow contrived to enlist the collaboration of such respected authorities as Graham Pollard, [2] Michael Sadleir, [3] the Printer to the University of Cambridge [4] and the Warden of All Souls. [5]

It is true that assistance in the compilation of the *ABC* itself is acknowledged not only to these same experts (once more) but also to such other reassuring names as John Hayward, H. M. Nixon, Percy Muir, A. N. L. Munby, Arnold Muirhead, Dudley Massey and Simon Nowell-Smith. Yet anybody can (and far too many authors do) attempt, by means of a few cheap prefatory compliments, to shift the responsibility for their own shortcomings on to the shoulders of distinguished persons who have been good-natured enough to oblige them with a couple of references.

In the present instance, it is clear that the author's long-suffering friends did much more than that. "There is not a paragraph," he says smugly, "which does not bear traces of their help." It may, indeed, be shrewdly suspected that such merit as is to be found in these pages—and there are, it must be admitted, passages which can be read without positive distaste—should be attributed to the gentlemen

[1] John Hayward, C.B.E.
[2] *An Enquiry into the Nature of Certain Nineteenth Century Pamphlets;* and *The Firm of Charles Ottley, Landon & Co., Footnote to An Enquiry* (Hart-Davis).
[3] *Victorian Fiction* (National Book League).
[4] *The Printed Book* (Cambridge University Press).
[5] *A. E. Housman, An Annotated Handlist* (Hart-Davis).

whose names adorn the dedication page and the preface, rather than to the author himself.

It must also, however, be admitted, albeit reluctantly, that there is a real need for a manual of this kind. It is seldom true to say of a book that "it fills a yawning gap"; but if Mr. Hart-Davis had said it of this particular book, full of ignorance and prejudice as it is, he could not be contradicted. The language of bibliography has many inflections beyond the scope of an ordinary dictionary. The even more private language of book-collectors—as anyone knows who has listened to two or three of these exotic characters talking shop—is thickly encrusted with jargon, special connotations and technical terms.

"Made-up," says one, with a sniff. "Q6 is a cancel as usual," says another resignedly. "My copy," says a third, with a complacent leer, "is an issue not recorded in GKW, with a dropped guide-letter on the privilege leaf." What is the ordinary man to make of such lingo as this? Mr. Hart-Davis, taking pity on him, would say "Buy a copy of *ABC for Book-Collectors* and look the word up." But although he is a collector himself, and undoubtedly means well, he can hardly be impartial about one of his own publications; and his advice will be taken with a pinch of salt.

Nevertheless, there is no doubt that a great many people *will* buy this book: for a number of reasons, mostly discreditable. Antiquarian booksellers, of course, will buy it to foist on their unsuspecting customers as propaganda. People interested in outlandish cults and esoteric rituals will buy it out of curiosity. People wanting a Christmas present for an uncle who is "a great reader" will succumb to the fallacy that book-collecting is connected in some way with literature, and the old boy won't like to send it back. People who hate book-collecting and despise collectors will buy it out of malice, as ammunition for ridiculing their bibliophile friends and catching them out on some technical point.

Novice book-collectors (the poor, credulous creatures) will fall on it with grateful cries, in thousands, under the fond impression that here, at last, is someone able and willing to tell them in plain language the meaning of all those weird terms which clutter up booksellers' and auctioneers' catalogues; to explain why books constantly described as rare sometimes seem so common, or why there is all this fuss about original boards; to elucidate the hundred and one other taboos and conventions which lend spice to their pursuit.

Finally, the experienced collector will buy it—not, of course, because he expects to find anything useful or informative in it, but on the contrary because he happily (and quite correctly) assumes that it will be full of idiotic mistakes which he will then be able to impale, with a withering comment, on a postcard to the author.

One would like to find *something* to commend in this foolhardy publication; and fortunately it is possible to praise without reserve both the sensible elegance of its production and the ingenuity of the numerous typographical gadgets with which Mr. Richard Garnett has enlivened the layout. It is, indeed, hardly too much to say that no classier piece of library-table decoration is likely to be available this season at the modest price of fifteen shillings.